TREKS
NOT TAKEN

What if Stephen King,
Anne Rice, Kurt Vonnegut, and other
literary greats had written episodes of
Star Trek: The Next Generation?

TREKS

NOT TAKEN

Steven R. Boyett

HarperPerennial
A Division of HarperCollins*Publishers*

Treks Not Taken is presented entirely as a work of parody. This book is in no way authorized by Paramount Studios or anyone owning rights in or to, or in any way connected with, the television series *Star Trek: The Next Generation*. Names of persons, institutions, and entities, real or fictional, are used in a parodic manner. All materials ascribed to other authors are in fact parodies of those authors written by the author of this book.

Originally published in August 1996 by Sneaker Press/Midnight Graffiti.

HarperCollins books may be purchased for educational, business, or sales promotional use. For information please write: Special Markets Department, HarperCollins Publishers, Inc., 10 East 53rd Street, New York, NY 10022.

FIRST EDITION

Designed by Elliott Beard

Library of Congress Cataloging-in-Publication Data

Boyett, Steven R.
    Treks not taken : what if Stephen King, Anne Rice, Kurt
  Vonnegut, and other literary greats had written episodes of
  Star trek, the next generation? / Steven R. Boyett. — 1st ed.
      p. cm.
  ISBN 0-06-095276-8
  1. Science fiction, American. 2. Star trek (Television program)—
Parodies, imitations, etc. I. Title.
PS3552.0896T7 1998
813'.0876208—dc21   98-18310

98 99 00 01 02 ❖/RRD 10 9 8 7 6 5 4 3 2 1

CONTENTS

CONTENTS

The Trekking
Not by Stephen King   135

Fandom Shrugged
Not by Ayn Rand   145

Holodeck-5, or, God Bless You, Mr. Roddenberry
Not by Kurt Vonnegut   153

Trek of Darkness
Not by Joseph Conrad   161

On the Bridge
Not by Jack Kerouac   171

Oh, the Treks You'll Take!
Not by Dr. Seuss   181

Acknowledgments   191

INTRODUCTION:
WHEN WORLDS COLLIDE

What if . . . ?

That question has been the driving force behind all great science fiction, on screen or in print. *What if books were outlawed?* (Ray Bradbury, *Fahrenheit 451*). *What if humanity had been created merely to serve an alien race's ends?* (Kubrick & Clarke's *2001: A Space Odyssey*; Vonnegut's *The Sirens of Titan*).

What if a United Federation of Planets mutually explored the galaxy?

What if the literary greats of our time had written episodes for *Star Trek: The Next Generation*?

It was with an odd mixture of sadness and accomplishment, pride and nostalgia, that the production offices of *Star Trek:*

The Next Generation closed shop after seven seasons and one hundred seventy-eight episodes. The original *Star Trek* series had a run of seventy-nine episodes; this "new and improved" incarnation had more than doubled it—and not merely in the number of episodes, but also in the production quality, sophistication, and often the subject matter of the stories themselves.

It was while cleaning out the production offices on the Paramount lot in Hollywood, soon after the completion of the show's final episode ("All Good Things . . ."), that a custodial staff member who shall remain anonymous discovered a dusty crate monogrammed with the Magic-Marker–scrawled initials *GR*. Curious, the custodian opened the crate and peeked inside—and the worlds of science fiction and literature found a rare intersection indeed.

The crate contained outlines for *ST:TNG* shows that were never produced.

Unproduced outlines were hardly a new discovery at *Trek;* custodians had been sweeping forgotten ones out from beneath desks for days now. What made *these* outlines so unique was their authorship: every one of them had been penned by writers famous in literary or popular circles, and sometimes in both.

Naturally the custodian (an aspiring scriptwriter, as are most menial workers in Los Angeles; without such hopefuls there would be no manual labor in this town) suspected a hoax. But, being of literary bent himself, he brought the crate to his modest apartment in the San Fernando Valley and began reading. And reading. And reading. And when he was done, he was convinced that he had in his hand the genuine articles.

How we came to acquire them is none of your business. And the custodian has since landed a promising gig with industry connections (he's a waiter at Le Dôme), so don't go looking for him, either.

In Hollywood, stories for episodic television are often sold on the basis of an outline. The writer meets with producers and/or the show's story editor, and "pitches" his story—tells it out loud in what he hopes is a dramatic and interesting fashion. If the production people like what they hear, the writer usually goes to outline to "firm up" the concepts and plot. To paraphrase Woody Allen, they have ideas that they firm up into concepts so they can go to outline to produce a story.

The question remains, then: If Gene Roddenberry (if indeed he is the GR of the scrawled monogram) had a crate full of outlines by such notable writers, why weren't these episodes ever produced? None of the other ST:TNG staff contacted even knew these outlines existed, much less why they had not been produced. The Great Bird of the Galaxy, as Roddenberry was affectionately known, had elected to keep them a secret.

Any explanation we can offer, then, is pure speculation. But speculation is the bread and butter of science fiction, and speculate we will.

Two observations:

1. *Star Trek* may be just a television show, but its universe and technology are complex, and as consistent as possible given the enormous collective effort it takes to produce a weekly TV series. Roddenberry may have insisted that *character* was the foremost consideration on his show, but the fact remains that the technological "backdrop" of *ST:TNG* was much more in the foreground than on nearly any other TV show. The stories were driven by ideas and technology, and writing them required a solid grounding in *Star Trek*'s dauntingly complex history, cosmography, xenology, terminology, and lots of other ologies. It took a certain kind of writer to create for the *Trek* universe.

2. Writers who have made a name for themselves, either critically or popularly (or, if they're among the exalted few, both), usually have done so because they have a unique way of looking at the world—their prose style is a distinctive voice (Salinger, Vonnegut, McCarthy), or their subject matter or pacing is one they have staked out for themselves (Clancy, Crichton, King). In a certain sense, how they write is who they are, and, for better or worse, their "flavor" can't help but come through in the reading.

Unmistakable distinction of narrative voice or theme is highly desirable in fiction. But when such writers try to create for such a TV show, the result is usually oil and vinegar: the flavor is unique, and you can clearly taste both ingredients, but they don't quite blend. Roddenberry was no doubt proud that such prestigious names desired to write for his show (though it is arguable many of *them* considered it a guilty pleasure), but as a producer he also would have been aware that his show could not *afford* a different flavor every episode. He couldn't have one show that dripped Stephen King and another that reeked of Jackie Collins. *Star Trek* had to scan like *Star Trek,* week after week, and these particular writers simply couldn't help sounding like themselves no matter *what* they tackled.

At the same time, and somewhat contrary to the above, it is an astonishing testament to the sheer versatility of *Trek* as a storytelling vehicle (figuratively and literally) that it *can* support such an amazingly broad array of styles and approaches. However varied—and even the casual reader will see that these outlines are *quite* varied—they still smell like *Trek*.

No doubt the Great Bird of the Galaxy regretted not being able to produce these stories. But no doubt he also kept them because he was flattered by them and fond of them.

Some of these outlines are purportedly written by authors who had been dead long before *ST:TNG* was a twinkle in its creator's eye: Conrad, Joyce, Hemingway, Melville. We know Roddenberry had a lot of influence, but surely not *that* much! Ruefully we concluded that, unless these stories had been transcribed during tabletop séances (a situation not remarkably different than a pitch meeting, come to think of it), these outlines were hoaxes, and we considered excluding them from this collection. But after voting on the issue we changed our editorial mind and left them in.

(Referring to ourself in the plural grants us such latitude.) Hoax or not, we reasoned, the episodes certainly *read* as if those writers had hitched their literary wagons to *Star Trek*. They may be fakes, but they're original fakes.

Finally, detail-conscious fans of *ST:TNG* will undoubtedly spot technical, historical, and biographical inconsistencies between these outlines and the televised show. We ask you to keep in mind that these outlines were written by authors who weren't necessarily conversant with the minutiae of the show—even those who might have been closet Trekkers. Also, these outlines, because they were unproduced, had not been reviewed by the *Trek* staff for consistency. We strongly feel that the aesthetic consideration of preserving these writers' work in the original form outweighs the compulsion to edit for conformity's sake.

As a lover of the written word and fan of *Star Trek: The Next Generation*, gentle reader, you can here appreciate the best of both worlds. So sit back in your reading chair with a steeping cup of relaxing hot tea beside you (Earl Grey, of course) and let us answer that question so fundamental to science fiction:

"What if . . . ?"

STEVEN R. BOYETT
BURBANK, CALIFORNIA

THE CRUSHER
IN THE RYE

Not by

J. D. Salinger

The first thing you'll probably want to know is what planet I was born on, and what life on a starship was like, and if I'm full human or mixed, and all that Roddenberrian kind of crap, but I'd just as soon not get into it, to tell you the truth. Besides, my mom's a doctor and all, and she'd probably give me a total diagnostic if I told anything personal about her.

So I guess I'll just tell you about this crazy stuff that happened to me on the *Enterprise* a couple months ago. The *Enterprise* had to be one of the crummiest places in the galaxy. You've never seen such a bunch of phonies in your life, really. Everyone on board is supposed to be so experienced and tops in their field—the best of the best, and all that. But I must have pulled their nuts out of the fire a dozen times. *Me,* a kid. Did anyone ever say, "Thank you, Wesden?" Not on your life. Ingrates. The ship was full of them.

Like this guy who was second in command, Wryker. We had an android on board who was more human than him! He thought he was such a hotshot because he was this incredibly good-looking guy with broad shoulders and a beard and all. Only everybody knew he grew the beard because without it, he looked just like that other legendary hotshot phony, Captain Jirk. The thing is that Wryker really was quite a hotshot, always giving the girls the time when he beamed down on shore leave. Then he'd come back grinning and passing around all these holos that were supposed to be naughty or something, only they were of him and some tramp who was so alien it was hard to tell which parts were supposed to be naughty. That's how it is with phony pervert bastards like Wryker. The *Enterprise* was full of them.

Anyway, the captain had called me into his ready room to say goodbye because I was leaving. I forgot to mention that. They kicked me out of the Academy. You've heard of the Academy. All it ever does is produce these clone Federation officers who all think alike. Believe me, they were all clones before they went in there. That's the way it is everywhere in the Federation. It's like there's a gene responsible for blandness, and they've isolated it. It's a terrible place any way you look at it, the Academy is.

It was my fault I got kicked out, it really was. I was a wingman of the goddamn Nova Squadron aerobatics team, if you can believe that, and we pulled a totally forbidden Kolvoord Maneuver around Saturn's rings that got this guy Josh killed. He was really a phony slob with rich phony parents, but we still shouldn't have done it, and there was a big inquiry and all, and the whole Academy ostracized me. It was supposed to be some big honor and ethics deal. It's a very ethical place, the Academy, it really is.

So I ran all the way to the captain's ready room on account

of I was so late. I've got no wind at all because I'm a child-prodigy wimp genius bookworm who's been coddled by his mom and everyone on board for as long as they let me fly the ship. They used to let me fly it, no kidding. Anyway, the captain was this really old guy without any hair and all, and I guess he felt bad because he's the one who made me confess at the inquiry or else he'd narc on me. He had no loyalty, the captain, none.

He was in his ready room drinking that totally pretentious Earl Grey tea, like it and his English accent would make up for the fact that he had a completely Frog name. What a complete phony. He was staring at his aquarium full of Magic Sea Monkeys that were just as phony as he was because everyone knows they're really just brine shrimp. When I came in he turned around and spoke to me in this very deep Shakespearean voice that was supposed to make me forget he was something like five feet tall. "Mr. Crushfield, I wanted to tell you goodbye before you leave us. I want you to know how badly I feel about your dismissal from the Academy."

"Yeah," I said, trying not to stare at his shiny head, "I know. But don't feel too bad about it. It was my fault, it really was. I should've known better."

"Yes, you really should have." This from the geezer whose life I saved about twelve hours before I reported to the Academy. It's just like I told you: ingrates.

I wanted out of there as fast as possible. One thing I hate, it's being lectured to in phony Shakespearean delivery by bald old short guys drinking tea. Like it's my fault he can't get the lead in *Lear*. He got all misty-eyed playing some really awful music on that cheap old beat-up flute of his while I sat there smiling and nodding. We talked about a bunch of stuff that doesn't matter, and then I told him I had to get back to my quarters and we shook hands. Real manly crap. Only he tried to crush my hand. That Academy training—I'm telling you, I didn't get out of there a minute too soon.

Instead of going to my quarters I went to Ten-Forward and tried to get Goynan to serve me a Kentucky rye. I mean, if a body wants a rye, why not come through for him? I know I look a lot older than I act, but she just laughed and served me one of those green-fluid malts. There are a lot of vitamins in green-fluid malts. That's me, ex-Ensign Vitamin Crushfield. "Hey, Goynan," I asked, mostly to show I wasn't sore because she wouldn't serve me alcohol, "you know those zooeybirds they got on Caulfield Seven?"

She wiped the counter with a spotless rag. "Sure, I know 'em. What about 'em?"

"Well, Caulfield's axis is at right angles to its sun and it's got a high rotation speed."

"Yeah, so?" She's very condescending, Goynan, she really is. Like a ship with food replicators really needs a bartender in the first place.

"So they get these crazy Coriolis winds and all during the winter. Like a thousand miles an hour. And I always wondered, where do the zooeybirds go in the winter?"

"How the hell should I know? What kind of question is that? You shouldn't even be in here. Let me see some ID."

"Look, just forget it, okay?" I got my malt and left. For someone with a cushy made-up job, Goynan could be touchy as hell sometimes. Serves me right for trying to make whoopie.

I grabbed a table over by the window and looked out at the stars and junk going by. What I was doing, I was trying to think up some kind of goodbye. When I leave a place, even a crummy one like the Academy or the *Enterprise,* I need some kind of goodbye. So I remembered this one time me and some of the mundane kids who weren't prodigies like me were playing tribble baseball on the holodeck. We just kept pitching and bashing for so long the ground got squishy. When the program made the sun go down I hacked into it and made it come back up and we made the afternoon last like twelve hours. I mean, we used up more tribbles than a fluffy-slipper factory.

Well, that was all the goodbye I needed. I drained my green malt and left Ten-Forward for good. And I was feeling pretty okay, I really was, and I meant to go straight to my cabin and sneak in without my mom noticing and grab my bags and all, and just transport right down to San Francisco, because I knew the town pretty good from when I went to the Academy like all the other square clones. I had a wad of dough they had to give me when I was dishonorably discharged, and I knew a couple places that would serve me. I planned to get pretty drunk and try to fall out the same window Jack Kerouac fell out of, and maybe find a couple girls I knew. I mean, one was a Vulcan and one was a Bajoran and all, but they were still *girls*, you know? And I really was going to head straight out of the *Enterprise* for good, only when I was headed down the corridor toward the turbolift I saw that somebody had sprayed *Frag the captain* on the wall in prismatic holopaint. Boy, one thing I hate, it's taggers. Don't even ask me about them. So I'm cleaning it off with a rag from my bags when the turbolift doors open and Lieutenant Wharf comes stalking toward me. He's this total hyperthyroid testosterone case, if you want to know the truth, and he sees me wiping the wall and he growls, "What are you doing?" He yanks me up and nearly breaks my arm, he grabs it so hard. So I try to explain that I'm wiping off this wall but Wharf interrupts me and explains that the captain had gotten worried after I left and he asked the computer where I was and it told him I was on Deck 7 scribbling on the wall. There's no privacy at all on the *Enterprise*. I mean, I could ask the computer what you were doing this very minute and it would tell me. I mean *anything* you were doing. It's a totalitarian state no matter how you look at it, the *Enterprise* is, and it's all run by goddamn moron jocks like Wharf. I couldn't wait to beam down.

Only I wasn't about to beam down, because Wharf found this can of holopaint in my bag that I'd forgotten all about, and he put two and two together (which is pushing it about as far as a Klingon can, but what do you expect from a pituitary case with a horseshoe crab on his head?). And so now they have a holo of me standing at the wall with my goddamn hand on this giant glowing *F* like I'd sprayed *Frag the captain* myself before leaving and I'm in hot water again. You may think you can leave a star vehicle like this, but you can't. And that's all I'm going to tell you about, Counselor. I know my goddamn rights.

A Clockwork Data

Not by
Anthony Burgess

M

ake it so, then, eh?"

There was me, that is Pickhard, and my three crew, that is Wort, Georgie, and Datum (Datum being really datum), and we sat in the *Enterprise* Ten-Forward synthobar making up our rassoodocks what to do with the episode, a rank flip Fall Sweeps bastard though wry. The Ten-Forward served Moloko Plus. That is, it served Molokos plus Klingons plus humans—in short, O my viewers, the Ten-Forward served anyone. You could peet it with synthehol or chase it with schnapps which would give you a nice quiet horrorshow fifteen minutes admiring the Big Window and All Its Hurtling Stars with lights bursting all over your sensors so that none of your words made any sense at all anymore.

The four of us were dressed in the height of Federation fashion, which in that season was a pair of black and red very tight tights with the old com insignia, as we called it, fitting on the chest in a sort of arrowhead design you could viddy clear enough was crasted from the Honda Acura logo. We wore our hair not too Nineties and we had flip horror-show phasers for shooting.

There were three Devotchkas at the counter all together, but none of us spoke Devotchkan and besides, we were with Datum. Datum was very malhuman and like his eemya he was a neo maxi geek dweeb, but he was a horrorshow officer and very handy with the keyboard.

"Make it so, then, eh?"

We had been gobbing all the doo-dah day about beam-beaming down to some starry old xeno's palatial domy and doing a bit of the old in-out to the Prime Directive like. Old Wart was always boohooing about not being allowed to lay on the old ultra-violence all about the malenky old *Enterprise,* so this nochy I messeled we could play the old Feddie millicent part to the hilt and go all a-trekking in fine fashion so Wart could have a dobby bit of Klingon fun.

We goolied along the corridor toward the beam-beam room. On the way I cracked this ensign veck on the cakehole and he doubled up and got all shaky and poogly. "What ever is the matter with our shipmate Barclay here?" Datum inquired in a real polite type goloss. "It seems he needs a leg up, eh?" And Datum hauled off and clopped this weepy chelloveck in the gluteus maximally with his hard android noga. And smecking like Cardassians we skatted on into the beam-beam room.

All this time Georgie was letting off real horrorshow with bezoomny technospeak like "Quantum charge reversals in antiprotons in the magnetic injection stream create incremental imbalance in the matter/antimatter plasma conduits that, if left unaltered, will lead to a right horrorshow warp-core breach." I couldn't see his glazzies behind his viddy-visor, but I knew he was in the Land, all right.

Wort tolchocked the beam-beam chief in his rotty mick

litso and we set the controls all random like the way we always do. We goolied onto the platform and energized, and O my viewers the world got all sparkly and spangly and I saw Borg and All His Holy Assimilators. Me gulliver was throbbing and words tasted all merzky in me gob. But instead of doing the old beam-in beam-out at some starry old devotchka's domy, we found ourselves in an all-white mesto, and the only vesch besides ourselves we could viddy was this bolshy throne and on it this doddery fey schoolmaster-type veck wearing starry platties and a powdered-wig luscious glory and looking for all the world like the late great Ludwig van B.

"Hi hi hi there," he says, all smecky in a friendly type goloss. "Welcome to the Continuum, gentlemen."

Wort growled and skatted forward to crack his simpering weak gob, but this veck just raised his rooker and snapped his fingers and Wort went all statue like. "Now now now," this creeching old veck govoreeted, "that's no way to treat your benefactor." He let out this big shoomy smeck and then viddied me. "My name is Skew," he told me. "Thou art Jean-Alex Pickhard, and thou art a rank horror malchicki-wick indeed, *mon capitain*. I am here to teach thee a lesson."

He waved his veiny old rookers and suddenly I was back on the starry bridge of the *Enterprise* with Rooker and my droogs Datum and Georgie and Wort. Now this is the real weepy and like tragic part of the episode. "Captain," said Wort in a serious and official type goloss, "I am receiving a distress signal from the Federation cutter *Britva*."

I opened my rotter to ask him why should I care about

some grahzny millicent ship, but what comes out, O my viewers, is me asking the ship's position in a very concerned type goloss. Wort told me and I ordered us there at ultra skorry warp.

In a minoota Datum viddied up from his Ops station and I slooshied him telling that the bratchny Feddie ship was in beam-beam range and was about to meet our old droog the warp-core breach. I grinned and viddied forward to a right horrorshow july fourth on the bigscreen telly.

"Your orders, Captain?" First Off Rooker viddied me with a frowning rot and I wanted to creech for him to warp his orders right up his bolshy cal turboshaft, but what came out instead was an order to beam-beam those wretched millicents to our ship and put our shields up up up.

The rescue went all horrorshow and we got all these simpering chellovecks and ptitsas safely on board before the *Britva* lit up all horrorshow and went to join the Great Borg of Ships in the Sky. Counselor Toy, this Betazed mozg-leech with bolshy groodies and an empathic rassoodock, govoreeted in this husky type goloss that I had done a radostyful deed and a great and wonderful vesch. This made me so razdraz that I lifted a rooker to shlaga her nuking litso, but instead I slooshied to my own goloss say, "Thank you, Counselor," all radosty and proper like.

All the rest of that shift was just as razdrazzing, O my viewers, with me govoreeting all shilarnied official and loveydovey and appy polly loggying for every stinking vesch I did. It was now my job to *avoid* dratsing and *save* bolshy merzky planets and shake rookers with stinking gloopy xenos—if they *had* rookers, that is—and very skorrily I went all bezoomny in me bald eggiwegg gulliver and viddied myself doing good deeds and proper vesches for the rest of my poor jeezny, and getting not a single piece of cutter or ptitsa for all my bolshy captainy efforts.

Pretty soon I ponied that all this chepooka was the doing of that starry old Skew bratchny, and in the middle of the bridge I started creeching and boohooing for him to make it stop. "I've learned me lesson, brother," I speechified. "I've seen the error of me ways! I've reformed, I tell you! I'm a whole new veck!"

By now the crew was viddying me with wide glazzies and the emdee, a schwoopy redheaded ptitsa, was jammiwamming a hypo into my pletcho to fill my mozg with drencrom and make me all spatty and drowsy like, and every vesch began to feel all beaming like around me and I slooshied the Ninth, the glorious Ninth of Ludwig van B, and I was back in the all-white mesto with grahzny old Skew still wearing his composer platties and showing his zoobies at me. "And what have you learned from all this, *herr kapitan?*"

I hugged his noga like a lubbilubbing dog. "That everything I need is right here," I platched. "And that I don't need to viddy farther than my own backyard, because there's no mesto like domy!"

He shook me off his noga all disgusted like. "Puh-*leeze!*" he creeched. "Thou canst can do better than that, Jean-Alex."

17

I messeled for a minoota, feeling very gloopy like. "I learned," I tried again, "that the old ultra-violence is—is wrong! That the Prime Directive is sacred! That Starfleet is a right horrorshow outfit, and that all messelling life-forms are droogs!"

His litso got all horrified looking and he held up his rookers. "No no *no!* That's not the lesson at *all!*" He leaned forward and narrowed his glazzies and said in a whisper type goloss, "The lesson is that it is better to *choose* to be evil than to have blandness *thrust* upon you."

I viddied him a long minoota and then I nodded me gulliver. The old malchick was right. Right as rain, right as dratsing, right as flowing purple Klingon krovvy. I would rather be baddiwad and have character than be dobby and have none. I turned and there was my old crew-droog Wort, still all statue like, and I goolied up to him and gave him a wide smecking grin and tolchocked him right in his hairy Klingon yarbles.

I was cured.

ONE BEAMED ONTO THE CUCKOO'S NEST

Not by
Ken Kesey

We're out here. Exploding strange new worlds. Boldly glowing. Security officers in bumblebee suits waiting for me to do something wrong. But I'm just a bit player on this ship and I don't have much to say, so everybody acts like they've forgotten I can talk at all. They just stare at me and say "Energize," and then they sparkle and fade. Once I got patted on the back by an admiral. "Yeah, you the Transpotah Chief, ain't that right, O'Brienden?" I feel like an extra.

I'm swabbing the deck outside sickbay when I hear a hiss, and Big Bev slides through the doors with her hair the color of the tip of a soldering laser. She's clutching her medikit as she hurries past. It's admission day. I'm still swabbing when Big Bev comes back with two security officers on either side of a man wearing a knit cap. He's small but he sounds big, like he's way above everybody. "So, this is the famous ward-ship *Booby Prize*, huh? *Very* impressive, Nurse Crusher!"

Her flinty eyes narrow and throw off sparks. "We don't use terms like that here, Mr. McPicard. This is a Federation mental-health vessel."

He just grins like she told a funny joke. "Oh, I don't stand on ceremony, Nurse Crusher. Call me J.P." The way he says her name it comes out "nuts crusher."

Big Bev's face turns into duranium. "Come along, Mr. McPicard. Time for your medication."

J.P. washes down his pill with Earl Grey tea and comes over to the Holorec Room where Kernel Data, one of the Chronics, is playing poker with La Phorge, one of the Acutes. Chronics are machines with flaws inside that can't be repaired, or at least they think they are. Acutes just have a complete lack of affect. La Phorge lays down a three and a King like he has a pair. La Phorge sees things the rest of us can't, and Big Bev lets him wear a pair of wraparound ski goggles he says help him out.

McPicard watches them, then grins and holds out his own deck of cards. "You want to see a real holo-deck?" he says, and fans them. I can see from where I'm standing there's pictures of naked Andorian ladies doing things with Cardassian rat-mules you can only do in low gravity. But they just ignore him and after a minute McPicard looks disgusted and goes to where Willie Wiker is trying to hide in the corner. "How about you, friend, what's your name?"

Wiker flinches like a cornered rabbit. "Wuh-wuh-wuh-*Will!*" he pops out.

J.P. sticks out a hand. "You a puh-puh-*poker*-playing man, Will?"

Big Bev is standing behind J.P. now. Her hair is glowing bright red. "Mr. McPicard, you're disturbing the crew. This is their off time."

J.P. ignores her. He sees me standing there and hurries over. "How about you, Chief? Just a round of fizzbin. Credit a point." I pretend like I haven't heard, and he just looks disgusted. "What's the matter with all of you?" he addresses the room. "What kind of men are you to be subjugated and kept down like this? What kind of chickenshit outfit is this, anyway?"

"You seem to be quite an orator, Mr. McPicard," says Big Bev. "Perhaps we can give you something to talk about." She has a crafty smile that worries me. When Willie Wiker first came on board, he had a lot of life in him just like J.P. But Nurse Crusher just got that crafty smile, and one day Will was ordered down to the Eveready Room, and the next day he came back acting just as stiff and wooden and lifeless as the rest of us.

Soon after, Kernel Data got into an argument with Nurse Crusher because he wouldn't take his medication. "I am a machine," he insisted, "and do not need medication."

"This pill will make you work better," the Nurse soothed. "It's a lubrication pill."

Kernel Data flexed his arms and legs. "I am functioning within normal parameters," he announced.

Big Bev got exasperated and glanced at McPicard. He just went on playing solitaire with his porno holo-deck. It looked like a miniature orgy was being held on the table in front of him. He'd been sullen ever since Nurse Crusher refused to let him see the world Sirius on the viewscreen. "Kernel Data," she said coolly, "you are not a machine, you are a man, and you will take your medication."

"Nothing makes *me* feel more like a man," came J.P.'s booming voice, "than a good old-fashioned Away Team mission." He clapped his hands and rubbed them together. "How's about it, Beaverly? You can make it so."

Even Willie Wiker brightened at that. "Awuh-awuh-away Team?" he sputtered.

That night J.P. roused everybody off their bunks. "All right, crew," he said, "everyone up. Come on, Chief, rise and shine." He got us all up and into our uniforms. "I got me two women in the service professions coming to take us on an Away Team mission," he announced. None of us believed him until he wedged open the pneumatic ward door and we saw the two women standing there. One was a barfly named Iguanan who dressed like a Rigelian lampshade, but who brought along a lot of booze she said she'd liberated. The other one was a nurse like Nurse Crusher, only her name was N. Deanna and she had great soft-looking breasts.

Behind them in the corridor, the security officer was passed out with a half-empty bottle of Romulan brandy beside him. I picked it up and guzzled it, then belched. *"Pardonnez-moi,"* I said.

"Funny, Chief," said J.P. "I thought they told me you were Irish."

The moment Will Wiker got a look at N. Deanna he started getting all flustered and said he couldn't guh-guh-go on no Away Team muh-muh-mission with no guh-guh-girl. But J.P. just put him next to her and snuck everybody into the main shuttle bay, and before you knew it we were heading away from the ship and Kernel Data was flipping it the finger. We let Jeordie fly the shuttle because of the extra colors he claimed he could see. J.P. grinned in the copilot's seat. "Sometimes a great notion requires great planning," he said. He glanced back. "William! There's a private room for you and N. Deanna in back. Show her that they lied when they named you Wee Willie Wiker!" He chortled and slapped Jeordie's knee.

We arrived back on the *Enterprise* fit and tanned. We'd gone fishing, and darned if La Phorge hadn't seen right into the water and snagged as many fish as the rest of us put together! Then we went gambling on Vega and Kernel Data won a fortune at blackjack till the casino kicked him out for counting cards even though they couldn't prove it. We had spent all of Kernel's money and we were laughing and pouring synthehol all over each other as the shuttle docked, but when the door opened and we saw Nurse Crusher standing there with two bumblebee uniforms behind her holding phasers and straps, everybody got real quiet.

Everybody but J.P., that is. He stepped right off that shuttle and gave Big Bev a hug like she was an old girlfriend. "Beverly!" he sang. "How is my carrot-topped Florence Nightingale? What say we sneak off to the Engine Room and have ourselves a power coupling?"

Big Bev saw Willie Wiker with N. Deanna the whore passed out on his lap and lipstick all over his face. Willie grinned and waved. "Howdy, Doc," he called. "This here's my special friend N. Deanna!"

"William!" she said sharply. "What would your father say?"

"My fuh-fuh-father?"

"Don't you know you're his Number One? Every time Kyle visits he tells me that. But now look at you! You know what you look like to me?" Her eyes narrowed but she still smiled. "Number Two! That's what you look like!"

"Nuh-nuh-nuh—"

"Belay that!" J.P.'s voice was commanding. "You're Number One, William! You're first, always remember that!"

Nurse Crusher smiled at J.P. "Why, Mr. McPicard. I have some sad news for you, I'm afraid. In your absence, we completely ran out of our supply of Earl Grey tea."

That was when J.P. jumped off the shuttlecraft and landed on top of Big Bev.

I was awake the night they brought him back from the Eveready Room. For the longest time I thought he was just pretending because he was a pretty good actor, better than the rest of us. But after a while I saw that he wasn't faking it. His posture was stiff and awkward, like ours. He tugged his uniform top every ten seconds on the dot, just like the rest of us. His voice, when he spoke, was a colorless monotone, and all he could say was technical jargon. Everything about him was wooden and lifeless and stiff. He didn't look big anymore, because he didn't act big. They'd made him regulation like the rest of us.

The stars were streaming past the wardroom windows as I crept across the room to his biobed. Silently I reached down, and got a good, firm grip, and even though he'd paid his dues like the rest of us, I terminated his commission.

La Phorge sat up from his bunk, and I realized he could see us even in the dark. But all he did was nod. "You done good, Chief," he said. "You done good."

I stole a shuttlecraft and headed out. I might go to the Neutral Zone, or maybe get a real job on Deep Space 9.

JURASSIC TREK

Not by
Michael Crichton

B y the late twentieth century, it had become embarrass-ingly obvious that no adventure of even remotely con-temporaneous dimensions could be related in a fictional set-ting without certain basic components. These components are: (1) a general, academic-sounding introduction; (2) con-stant departure from the action to provide lengthy explana-tory narrative sections; and (3) heavy reliance on footnotes, charts, quoted (and often fictive) scholarly works, and graphs.[1] By the mid-twenty-fourth century, it had become impossible to tell even an hour-long story without employ-ing these narrative devices and several others, including

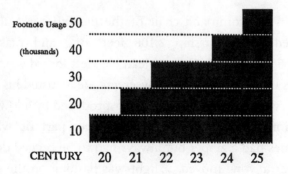

---

[1]Graph from "Footnote-Usage Ratios in Technoliterature," by T. Clancy, Patriot Press.

two-dimensional characters defined entirely by their job description; systemic breakdowns described by cutting-edge mathematical models mouthed by characters who are androids or might as well be; wholly artificial and contrived "ticking clocks" employed to add suspense; and the nondramatic resolution of the overwhelming majority of problems through the use of computers.

In this tradition, then, one could not depict a more perfect model of such a techno-thriller mission than the "Jurassic Trek" incident of Stardate 48175.15. The author would like to thank Lt. Commander Geordie La F_____ and Captain Jean-Luc P_____ for their kind, generous interviews, and Starfleet Headquarters for its generous support in providing access to recently declassified Federation documents.

+ 12:01:32

Seated in the command chair of the *Enterprise,* a Galaxy-class Federation starship 2,108 feet long and massing 5,000,000 metric tons, Captain Jean Hewlett-Picard watched the stars hurtle toward the viewscreen. He adjusted his uniform, a two-piece synthetic polymer produced by a low-bid Federation defense contractor, the upper part of which sometimes had a zipper but always had to be tugged down whenever anyone moved. A light was flashing on the console beside him and he glanced at it.

FLASH FLASH FLASH FLASH FLASH FLASH

Later on, Hewlett-Picard would admit he had thought the flashing light was unimportant. Since this regrettable incident, Starfleet has expended Cr. 5,827,322.87 to add a tone to accompany such alerts.

BEEP BEEP BEEP BEEP BEEP BEEP BEEP

From his ergonomically designed console, Lieutenant Commander Jetta, an android constructed by an independent contractor and supplied to the Federation in exchange for industrial-grade dilithium mined by genetically enhanced primates of the Lost Colony of Congoleum on the planet Zinj, reported that the ship was encountering a mysterious quasi-electromagnetic nonspectrum beam of neologistic origin. "This beam is bound to have an effect on the molecular structure of the ship's hull," warned Jetta.

"Explain," ordered the captain.

Chief Engineer Georgie La Porge took up the explanation. "As you know, sir, the *Enterprise* hull is constructed of pure sesquipedalium. It's a memory-metal that retains its basic shape despite severe stress. In theory, the ship could get all bent out of shape and still return to its proper form."

"Much like an expensive pair of antique titanium spectacles," Jetta elaborated helpfully for the sake of the audience.

"I see," said Hewlett-Picard. "I seem to recall reading a classified government paper on this subject."

Classified Personnel File:
Trite, Deanna (NMI)

ASSIGNMENT: U.S.S. *ENTERPRISE*

DUTIES:

1. Ask obvious questions to provide explanations to viewing audience

2. Intermittent love interest / threatened object

"So what's the problem?" asked Consoler Trite, a curvaceous yet bright empathic Betazed woman.

"The problem," replied Jetta, "is that the metal used in constructing the hull of the *Enterprise* was purchased from an unspecified low-bid contractor at secret government auction. This metal had a prior existence in a more primitive form. The neologistic energy beam we have encountered will cause the sesquipedalium to revert to its primordial forms."

"What are those forms, Mr. Jetta?"

Jetta tapped his computer console. A table appeared.

FUNCTN	PROBLTY (%)
TOASTERS	.37
CAN OPENERS	.37
REFRIGERATORS	.18
WIDGETS / DOORSTOPS	.18

"Our hull," the android continued, "will revert to those shapes, in proper percentages, of course, in exactly twelve hours."

12:00:00

Dr. Beverly "Number" Cruncher, a GP and field medic, was a shapely auburn-haired beauty, but she was also quite intelligent. She used a laser pointer to indicate the diagram on the electronic chalkboard. "Right now, our DNA strands are like a film being run in reverse—if we still used film, of course." They were in the briefing room, because lengthy expositional dialog scenes have to occur *some*where. "The neologistic beam has made our DNA behave like the molecular structure of the sesquipedalium. We're reverting. Over the next twelve hours we're going to devolve from humans to protohominids, to monkeys, and finally into spaceport baggage handlers."

"That's terrible," Hewlett-Picard exclaimed. "Baggage handlers?"

"It gets even worse." She tapped her keyboard and a new diagram appeared. "We'll then revert through all major mammalian stages, then probably reptilian."

"We'll turn into dinosaurs?" asked Commander Hacker, sounding excited.

Cruncher nodded. "Then into ferns. Then slime molds. Then amoebas. Possibly even lawyers."

"How can we be certain this will happen?" asked Hewlett-Picard.

"I read a classified government paper on the subject," said Dr. Cruncher.

Jetta nodded. "This is all predicted by chaos theory," he said.

08:32:17

In the end they fed all the information to the ship's computer and waited. Computers run 1.5 kerjillion times faster than the human brain, and are infinitely more interesting to write about. "I only hope the computer comes up with a solution before it reverts into an abacus," said Hewlett-Picard. "Right now it's become only as smart as a million accountants named Morty."

It took the computer 37.3 minutes to come up with a solution—the equivalent of $3,382^5$ minutes in people years.

07:56:09

The transporter was a sophisticated plot device that worked by beaming a bright light on an actor and then processing his image in a special-effects lab so that he faded out of a plywood backdrop and faded into an exotic alien matte painting.

"Energize," said Hewlett-Picard.

03:13:18

The transporter retained on file a molecular template of all who used it, so that any deep-structure biological flaws—

congenital mitochondria mutation, neologism-beam reversion of DNA structures, or writerly aspirations—could be corrected at the most fundamental level. The *Enterprise* crew had to hurry before the transporter devolved into a New York taxicab.

The crew beamed onto a nearly believable planetary soundstage. Cruncher's medical tricorder verified that they were all right. The crisis was averted. Tension abated. The clock ran out.

"Good work," said Hewlett-Picard.

00:00:00

Orbiting around the computer-generated planet was a cloud of toasters, can openers, refrigerators, and widgets/doorstops that had been the *Enterprise*. Lieutenant Commander Jetta had remained on board in a last-ditch effort to solve the problem. After devolving through increasingly primitive incarnations as a Vulcan science officer, an abortive TV series character named Questor, and an arched Philco radio, Jetta ultimately reverted to a wooden marionette with a long nose and dressed in a feathered cap and an odd Alpine outfit. His loss was felt in unquantifiable emotional terms.

BIBLIOGRAPHY

Crichton, M., *The Compilation of Fictive Bibliographical Sources*, 1996, from
    Pseudonymonthly, 1, no. 1 (inaugural issue) 1965, ed. John Lange.

Goldman, W., *Expand Your Film Outline into a Lucrative Novel*, 1988, self-published, n.d.

La Forge, G., "Hull Structure Schematics and Memory-Metal Polymers, with Additional Notes on Technical-Sounding Terminology, AKA 'Trekolalia'," *Starlog*, 4401.12

Sternbach, R., and M. Okuda, *Star Fleet Technical Manual*. New York: Pocket Books, 1991.

Trout, K. "Camouflaging Science Fiction Stories for the Mass Market Readership," *Writer's Digest*, 9, no. 5.

THE SHIP ALSO RISES

Not by

Ernest Hemingway

On the southern hemisphere of the planet N-gaje N-gai there is a shrine built on the snowy western summit of an extinct volcano. The shrine is carved from living rock and depicts a slight, bald humanoid holding a weapon in one hand and a pair of pointed ears in the other. The shrine is constructed above the 6,000-meter line, which on this world is unbreathable and unbearably cold.

Federation scientists discovering the shrine in the thirtieth century asked the primitive natives who could have built it at that altitude and what it depicted. The natives merely shrugged and recited a garbled speech that had been taught to their fathers and their fathers' fathers and their fathers' fathers' fathers. The universal translator determined the speech to be from King Lear, *by William Shakespeare.*

ook at them," he said. "Sitting off our bow like vultures. Now is it visual contact or is it sensors that brings them like that?"

"Don't. I sense danger."

The chair the captain sat on was in the center of the wide bridge and as he looked out at the viewscreen there were three of the big warbirds floating obscenely.

"They've been there since the inertial dampers broke down. I watched the way they decloaked in case I ever wanted to describe it in a bar on shore leave. There's an irony in the fire."

"I sense your frustration."

"I'm going to deliver a soliloquy. It's much easier if I soliloquize."

"I wish you wouldn't, Captain. It makes me very nervous to just sit here on the bridge, mission after mission, and not do anything. We might as well make it easy as we can until the commercial break comes."

"Or until the commercial break doesn't come."

"Please tell me what I can do. There must be something I can do. I'm under contract; they have to pay me for the episode. You might as well make use of me."

"What about a drink?"

"I'm ship's counselor, not a maid."

"Dworf!"

"Yes cha'Dich."

"Bring Earl Grey!"

"Yes cha'Dich!"

He stood from the command chair and looked at the viewscreen where the huge, filthy Rumulan warbirds sat, their naked disruptors displayed obscenely.

So it's come to this, he thought. Now he would never collect residuals on four centuries of Pontiac commercials. Now he would never again trample grapes in Robert's fine vineyards or drink the wine that came from them, the good wine, the '47. Now a minute fluctuation in the inertial dampers had left him motionless and drifting and unable to fight back against the filthy Rumulan *Polanski*-class ships. Now he would never again urinate long and hard and proudly against the old wall of the Prime Directive, never play Lear in the New Old Globe on Nova Avon.

"Another fine mess you've got us in."

He turned at the voice of his first officer. "What did you say?"

"I said another five minutes and they'll do us in."

Together they watched the warbirds. The Rumulans could smell the *Enterprise* dying.

"Captain, may I make a suggestion?"

"Yes Mr Feta."

"The planet we are currently orbiting is Class M. The large southern continent is primarily open savannah inhabited by mammalian predators and grazing beasts. It is an excellent hunting ground."

"Now is not the time to discuss hunting game, Mr Feta."

"My suggestion was not to hunt game, Captain. You know the Rumulans have a highly developed warrior code which they call *mah-choh*. Under the rules of *mah-choh*, if you were to personally challenge the leader of the Rumulan vessels—"

"Personally? Single combat? *Mano a Rumulo?* Hand to hand and tooth and claw, our meaty hearts pumping and the blood singing in our veins at the awesomeness of life that close to death?"

"Something like that, sir."

"Captain, I can't let you do it," said Riter. "It is my responsibility to lead Away Team missions. And, quite frankly sir, I look much better in khaki and a snap-brim."

Ship's Counselor D'yanna Tryst looked at William Riter quickly. She was an extremely ample and decorative woman who had served under Riter years ago and could not help but surrender to his overwhelming magnetism and testosterone reek.

"This is not an Away Team, Mr Riter," the captain said. "A man has to do what a man has to do."

"Sir—"

"I *must* go Number One."

"It's right down the hall sir."

He beamed down to the alien plain and the afternoon was hot and the day was good and in the distance rose a snow-topped mountain and Captain Picador stood with his phaser ready, hearing the filthy *maricon* Rumulan stamping about in the veldt with his smell of war and *mah-choh* and Aldebaran whiskey-soda, and the short happy man clenched his other fist and called out his soliloquy in a strong and steady voice with good gravel underneath, declaring, "By my troth, I care not; a man can die but once; we owe God a death and let it go which way it will, he that dies this year is quit for the next." And from the bush the Rumulan growled his speechless frustration and Picador saw the swishing rush in the grass and he raised his arm and the phaser phased and Picador picked his shot and fired; but the Rumulan kept on coming with his pointed ears flat to his head. Picador shot again and saw the charge de-fur a feline behind the Rumulan and he knew there was more than one way to do that. He shot again and he heard the charge hit, and the Rumulan, horrible-looking now, with half his satanic head seeming to be gone, crawled toward Picador in the edge of the tall grass while the bald-faced man smelling death in the afternoon worked the setting on the short ugly phaser and aimed carefully as another blasting *frrrzat!* came from the muzzle, and the crawling, alien bulk of the Rumulan stiffened and the huge, mutilated head slid forward.

The captain pulled out his vibro-knife and awarded himself two ears and a tail.

Commander Riter found the captain's comm insignia beside the stiffening body of the Rumulan. The Rumulan's flanks were very wet and his ears were very bobbed and flies were on the cauterized meat the phaser blast had made of his latex hide.

He gave the insignia to Lt. Dworf. "Without this on his uniform we'll never find him."

The tall black warrior said nothing, but he clenched the insignia in his very large and very callused hands and gazed out at the snow-covered mountain rising in the far distance.

LESS THAN DATA

Not by

Bret Easton Ellis

No one ever merges on the transporter. I am thinking about that when I beam back to the *Enterprise* after my shore leave, that it is good that no one merges on the transporter, but no one ever mentions it, even to say that it is good. In my cabin I plug my head in and slam some current until a good buzz gets going. Then I go to the holodeck and watch holos for a while, but after a few hours I realize nothing interesting is playing and my buzz is gone, so I plug my head in and scarf up some more juice and decide I will go to the bridge to see what is going on. The turbolift is waiting for me the way it is always waiting for anyone who wants to use it no matter where on the ship they are. "Bridge," I tell the turbolift, and on the way up I feel stupid for talking to a machine until I realize that I am a machine and that only makes me want some more current. I have no recollection of last night, either because I had too much intake or not enough, or possibly because there is no night on the *Enterprise*. All of this seems irrelevant next to that one word, "Bridge."

I am on the bridge and no one looks at me come in and I wonder if I were on the bridge watching myself come in would I look. Everyone is watching the viewscreen but after a few hours I realize there is nothing interesting showing so I go to my science station and plug my head in and set the impedance for maximum. The Science I station is an undiluted source and I get a charge out of that. Lieutenant Worfarer is looking at me strangely and I try to remember if I have slept with him and then I remember that I do not sleep at all. Worfarer looks annoyed but then he always looks annoyed, but just to be polite I ask him what is wrong and he just growls. "You look pale," he says.

I bring Worfarer and Geordache to the Ten-Forward Lounge and Worfarer drinks a drink with something swimming in it and Guinian pours Geordache a shot of Centauri Rye, only she pours short because Geordache cannot see a damn thing with those wraparound Ray-Bans over his eyes. He never takes them off, rain or shine, day or night. He says they make him see colors the rest of us cannot and I tell him I hope that extra colors and looking trendy make up for getting cheated on his synthehol ration. I plug my head into a jack at the bar to maintain my current affair and my buzz comes back and we turn at the bar to watch the lights going by in the observation window and after a few hours we realize nothing interesting is streaming past so we get more drinks and current. Worfarer asks me do I remember him getting smashed last night and pats his forehead gingerly. Pretty smashed, all right, says Geordache. I think Geordache is worried about Worfarer but it is difficult to tell because Geordache is wearing those Ray-Bans and the rest of his face never has any expression at all and neither does his voice. I look around the room and wonder if Geordache and Worfarer have slept together. Then I wonder if Geordache sleeps, and if he does does he leave the lights on, or does he keep his eyes open, or can he close the little designer venetian blinds in his Ray-Bans?

"What?" I ask when Geordache calls my name for what is probably the third or fourth time. I look past him at Worfarer looking concerned and I say what again.

"I said, So what have you been doing?"

"Oh." I look around. The stars are still streaming from the window. Guinian has cut Will Slacker off because he is a couple sheets to the solar wind and he wants to keep playing darts, only he keeps aiming at the window. At the other end of the bar is Ensign Barcode looking tweaked as usual and he's using a pocket laser to burn graffiti onto the counter top. "Just shocking myself," I tell Geordache, and I plug my head jack back into the bar outlet. The current lights up my positronic brain and I think, *Engage.*

"Me and Worfarer, we're worried about you, Datameister." He calls me that, Datameister.

"Who, me?"

"You look pale," Worfarer says from on high. It seems I have heard him announce this before but I cannot determine the exact time. Worfarer raises his glass and drains it and whatever was wriggling around in there goes into his mouth too and Worfarer gargles loudly, just to annoy it I guess, and then he swallows. I am thinking that he really does look a lot like Gene Simmons.

I look at Worfarer's deep dark skin and Geordache's rich deep complexion and I hold up my hand and see that he is right. I am pale. "Well," I say.

"We could go to my cabin," says Worfarer. "I have just the thing for you."

So we all go to Worfarer's cabin and I get wired on current Geordache has polarized in some exotic way. We turn on Worfarer's cabin viewer and watch the stars for a couple of hours but as usual there is nothing interesting on. Worfarer opens a tube of epidermal pigment that is illegal on Earth, which is why it is called Banned de Sol, and he takes off my uniform and rubs the pigment all over me and then Geordache takes off his uniform and says he would like to request a transfer to a Data-entry position. I watch the stars go by and wonder if I will ever remember last night or ever even find out if there was a night at all.

Later I realize I am in the Ten-Forward again and I am half fried on current and I have no idea what time it is but all the customers are gone and Guinian is the only one here besides me and I realize that I have decalibrated my internal chronometer and I look at Guinian and say "I have decalibrated my internal chronometer." Who hasn't? she says without looking at me. Beneath me on the counter top are burn marks where someone with a pocket laser has written RED ALERT RED ALERT RED ALERT in textbook Parker-penmanship letters and I try to remember who I saw writing it earlier but I am unable to, and that makes me realize that it has finally happened, I have overdosed on current and am a burnout, a shell of a man fried beyond repair, and I want to cry but I am a machine and not able to cry and the fact that I am unable to cry makes me want to cry and I think about how much better I would feel if I could get reprogrammed just enough to be able to use contractions or maybe even just a comma every now and then.

TREK-22

Not by

Joseph Heller

It was a horrible duty, but Doc Crasher didn't laugh until Rekker came to her one mission and pleaded to be released from his contract. Doc Crasher snickered but was also immersed in problems of her own, including why her hairstyle appeared different every week and why she couldn't get any medical readings on the dead man who wasn't in Comm. Data's cabin.

"You're wasting your time," Crasher told Rekker.

"You can't release someone who wants to resign?"

"Oh, sure. I have to. Especially if their performance is bad enough. There's a paramount clause that says I have to release anyone whose performance is bad enough."

"Then why don't you release me? My performance is *terrible*. Just ask Sheordie."

"Sheordie? But Sheordie's performance is terrible."

"Then why don't you release him?"

"I'd be glad to. But first he has to convince me his performance is awful and he wants to be let go."

"Then you can release him?"

"No. Then I can't release him."

"You can't release him?"

"TREK won't let me."

"TREK?"

"The Termination of Redundant *Enterprise* Kilotonnage. Trek-22 we call it. Anyone who can convince me they can't perform is by definition a capable performer."

There was only one trek, and that was Trek-22, which specified that terrible performance on a continuing mission was sufficient reason to be released from contract. Sheordie's performance was terrible and he could be released. All he had to do was convince Doc Crasher he was terrible and she could release him. But as soon as she was convinced, Sheordie had put on a good performance and wasn't bad enough to be released. Sheordie's performance was bad if you were aware of his performance. But once he demonstrated that his performance was as unexceptional as nearly everyone else on board, he was good and had to stay on.

Rekker was deeply moved by the absolute simplicity of this paramount clause and let out a respectful whistle. "That's some trek, that Trek-22."

"Best there is."

It reminded Rekker of the fires in Comm. Data's wires. "Data," he'd whispered as they'd passed each other in a corridor, "you've got fires in your wires."

"Beg pardon, sir?" Comm. Data cocked his head like the RCA dog.

"You've got fires," Rekker repeated, "in your wires. That's probably why you can't detect them."

Comm. Data had some time ago angered the BjörnBorg by covertly selling them faulty used machine parts he had originally stolen from them without knowing they were faulty, and he had had to arrange for the *Enterprise* to secretly attack a Federation outpost so that the BjörnBorg would not retaliate for buying their own faulty machinery parts by openly attacking the Federation outpost. He went to soon-to-be-ex-Captain _____-Luc Picard. "Captain," he queried, "do I have fires in my wires?"

The captain looked up from lengthy reports he had not signed with someone else's name in someone else's handwriting, reports he was unofficially not sending to Admiral Bull at Strawfleet because the admiral had ordered him not to send many more communiqués than he was currently not sending. Every admiral in Strawfleet was so phenomenally incompetent they had all been promoted to admirals. "Liars?" the captain asked.

"No, fires. In my wires, sir."

"Mr. Data, how can you be equipped to perceive fires in your wires if you have fires in your wires?"

"That's what Mr. Rekker told me, sir."

"Rekker? He was probably just putting you on."

"But I would have detected such a deception, sir. Mr. Rekker is not a capable performer."

"Yes, I've just failed to read the unofficial report I haven't received from Doc Crasher on his abilities. It's why I can't release him from his contract. Now you, Comm. Data, you've performed admirably. I'll be sorry to see you leave."

"But I am a regular crew member, sir."

"With fires in your wires? I should hope not. And certainly not until I've completed my investigation into the dead man who isn't in your cabin."

The dead man who was so conspicuously absent was a source of consternation for Doc Crasher, who had given Comm. Data a clean bill of health and therefore released him from his contract during an exam in which Comm. Data had complained about failing to receive negative results on his cognitive abilities whenever he performed a Level I diagnostic on himself. "If I do not get negative results, how can I trust that I am thinking properly?" Comm. Data had complained. "The more flawless the results, the more certain I become that the diagnostic program is faulty. In fact, no diagnostic program is perfect; therefore, I must be seriously flawed."

"I don't know," Doc Crasher had said. "But I can't find your pulse, your respiration is zero, and your blood pressure is nothing over nothing."

"But I am a machine," Comm. Data had responded.

"Well, Strawfleet medical regulations state that crew members with no heartbeat, respiration, or blood pressure are legally dead, and I can't authorize legally dead crew members for active duty."

Doc Crasher had filled out a death certificate which Comm. Data had refused to sign because his signature would acknowledge he was dead even though if he was dead he couldn't sign it. Strawfleet required the subject's signature on all death certificates for reasons of legal liability. They were afraid of being sued by someone who was legally dead but who had been pronounced otherwise. Comm. Data had retired to his cabin to figure out what to do. A security team had arrived to take his dead body for burial, but they had been puzzled when Comm. Data had told them there was no dead body there. Doc Crasher had run a full scan and it had come up negative, which was to be expected because dead men didn't show up on scans. If the scan detected nothing then that meant it was not reading a body that was most definitely in Comm. Data's cabin, but no one could find it.

Everyone at the funeral puzzled how a body could not be there when it was dead and couldn't go anywhere. Watching everyone crying at Comm. Data's funeral, Rekker puzzled most of all. He put a consoling arm around Comm. Data because everyone was rudely ignoring the android because they didn't want to be seen talking with a dead crew member. They were afraid they would be ordered to report to Doc Helenov Troy, the ship's psychiatrist, for evaluation. Doc Troy dispensed advice on parenting and social relations and remaining sane under spacefaring conditions. Troy hated her mother, had no children, got along with no one, and was crazy. She didn't even dress like anyone else on board. She made everyone uncomfortable.

"You'd have to be crazy to do her job," soon-to-be-ex-Captain _____-Luc Picard said. _____-Luc was a good captain whose only clue to the ship's direction was to look out the window of his ready room to see which direction the stars were streaking this week. It changed all the time: left-right, right-left, approaching, receding, up-down, down-up.

Comm. Data wasn't officially allowed to attend his own funeral service because he was deceased, but Doc Crasher had given him permission to be there because without him there wouldn't be a body that had been declared legally dead, and Strawfleet regulations required a dead life-form at all funerals. After the funeral everyone told Comm. Data how sorry they were that he was dead even if he never had actually been alive, and then they went to attend the court martial of soon-to-be-ex-Captain _____-Luc Picard for being a surgically altered Romular spy. He had been caught red-handed using the proper access codes to obtain top-secret information from the ship's computer. Since it was a spy's mission to obtain the proper access codes to steal secret information, and since the captain had them, he was probably a spy. The wrong access codes were no good to a spy, but the captain didn't use the wrong codes the way an innocent man would have.

Doc Crasher testified that _____-Luc Picard's surgical alteration was so perfect she could detect no evidence of it, and only the Romulars could perform such an alteration and leave no trace. Doc Troy testified that she had suspected _____-Luc Picard was a spy because he wasn't an incompetent like every other captain in Strawfleet. Doc Troy testified that she had suspected _____-Luc Picard was a spy because he wasn't a belligerent jerk like every other captain in Strawfleet. It was an open-and-shut case, and _____-Luc Picard was exonerated and given an Emmy and promoted to Admiral.

At the award ceremony Rekker drummed his fingers and sighed. *Tasha* had gotten out of her contract, for christ's sake, and she was utterly incapable of handling her security role. And Weasel Crasher. Yet every time Rekker and the rest of the cast used all their inconsiderable talents to perform terribly, their ratings improved and they had to fly more missions. They were never off *Trek*.

Rekker sighed. Where were the genes of yesteryear?

All the
Pretty Humans

Not by

Cormac McCarthy

The turbolift and the sound of the turbolift stopped with a soft sloughing and the doors hissed open for him to enter the bridge and hissed shut again when he had. The floor muted his nonhuman footfalls. In his trim mustardcolored Federation uniform the android stood on the bridge so palely looking at his crewmates working. He looked at Wyrp at his Security station. He looked across the curved expanse of railing. The baldheaded captain seated in his chair polishing his English tack saddle. To the captain's left and to his right, Counselor Troi Rogers and Commander Willie Rider. Lastly he looked at the viewscreen before them out of which hurtled blindwhite specks of gas accreted over aeons from the echo of their making as if the ship itself summoned their pinprick light from the increate dark ahead of it, white dwarf and red giant and contact binary, born of the act of forging through hyperspace itself, parsec on sector on quadrant filling the screen to sideslip by as if in passing all the matter of Creation were relegated to entropy, to history, to memory. Then he turned and went toward the captain. This was not flying. This was not flying.

The bald man looked up when the android stood before him. Yes Mr Dido?

Captain. One of our shuttlecraft is missing.

Missing?

My guess is the Vakerans we were conveying to Bamanos Two snuck by our security subroutines. I would be willing to bet my favorite Deadwood City holodeck program they erased any record of the craft being removed from the bay.

Which shuttlecraft, Mr Dido?

Rosinante.

Your favorite, wasn't it, Will?

Yeah. She's a good shuttle. He began rolling a cigarette.

How long ago, Dido?

Eleven hours, fifty-seven minutes. Give or take.

Rider spat on the deck. Out of sensor range by now. Hell, Cap'n, they're probably long gone across the Border Zone.

Very well, Number One. You and Mr Dido know what to do.

In the shuttlecraft bay Dido checked his phaser and the charge of his phaser and he checked the engines and the level of the dipsticks and he saw they all were full and that his phaser was set on stun and he returned it to its Velcro holster and saw to their provisions because who could say how long they might be gone or how far? Not man or god or computer or even space itself, for these are distances not measured by any tricorder or sensor, which was why the fullness of the phaser charge was so important a thing.

In the pilot's chair Rider powered up the console and stroked the controls with familiar hands and under his breath he spoke to the skittish craft in the way of men born to pilot machines, and he told the navigation console where they were going and what they were looking for and never did he doubt that the shuttlecraft understood, for such machines though not alive in the way men are alive or even in the way of animals or Merengi nonetheless share a common soul that was created for space travel by the will of men and never were these machines more alive than when they were ploughing the overwrought dark and led by the firm commands and hands of those who built them and knew them and loved them well.

Scout, you're cleared for departure. Soon as you cross the Border Zone you'll be on your own, Will.

Always was, Cap.

They flew all day into the eternal night continually losing and regaining the *Rosinante*'s ion trail leading into the Border Zone into which all men stared and few men dared for when they fared they came out scared from that place there. Rider set the autopilot and patted the console and spoke to it reassuringly in a language Dido thought unseemly as at the replicator he rustled up beans and Vegan tortillas and bitter Martian High Mountain coffee. Rider ate in silence while Dido watched his reflection in the forward port like the ghost of a machine. Soon Rider wiped his plate clean with his tortilla and flung his coffeegrounds in the replicator and Dido set the environmental controls to emit a soft muted crackle as of a campfire and Rider fully reclined his chair and slept covered by his thin electric bedroll while

Dido kept the watch, and while Rider slept he dreamed of ion trails in the cold vast reaches crossing and recrossing and nearly dispersed, the remnants of shuttlecraft passed long before, etheric disturbances of ancient battles hard-fought, and won, and disengaged, and as he tracked them with his Academy skills hardlearned he found them all, dozens of them capering, cavorting, nacelles alight and nosing and dodging, all the pretty shuttlecraft flying in that ether which is space itself and which cannot be spoken of but only written about to critical acclaim and prestigious awards.

He awoke to steady beeping and Dido's voice. The android was smoking a cheroot and staring out the port. Company, Commander.

He sat up. Who?

Merengi Marauder. Been hailing us.

On screen.

The grinning illsculpted face of an unwashed Merengi with crooked teeth filled the comm screen and Rider felt his own face go hard. He had in his time encountered many Merengi, and always his face went hard.

Ooday ouyay eeksay omulansray, umanhay?

Negative, Merengi, we are seeking a stolen shuttlecraft. Not Romulans.

The Merengi turned to one side and spat. Iarlay! Ouyay areyay pyingsay!

Amesay otay ouyay. End transmission.

Dido cut the signal. Commander, I got me a sensor ping shows a decaying warp-coil field signature just like what you would expect from a shuttlecraft engine turned off in the past ten or twelve hours.

That a fact? Rider spat. The *Scout*'s deck was by now slightly moist with expectorant. Where they stabling her, Mr Dido?

Cargo bay of that Merengi ship.

Open a channel.

When the Merengi appeared again Rider turned his head and spat. Merengi vessel, you are in possession of our stolen shuttlecraft. Now, I'm sure you didn't know no better when you bought it, but it was stolen from us all the same.

The peasant Merengi face turned to one side and spat. Oh, no, no! Ees no Federationale sheep! Ees Merengi shuttle. Merengi!

Then I guess you won't mind showing us your ownership papers.

The Merengi squinted and showed his crooked brown teeth. Papers? We don't got to show you any steenking papers!

Dido looked up from his console. They are powering up their weapons, Commander.

Eet ees a small thing, thees matter of a shuttlecraft. The Merengi made a brushing motion. What ees thees thing? Onay attermay. The Merengi told them it was not given for men to know the ways of shuttlecraft. He told them he himself had seen shuttlecraft that would not operate for men who sought them but would respond without complaint to those who claimed them. He said space was big and stars were many. He mentioned a dusty little moon he visited certain summers as a child. There was a one-eyed Norsican, a giant lizard, a bowl of bright green eggs. He quoted from the King James Bible and from Carlos Castañeda. He claimed the Federationales were Vakerans and had the souls of Vakerans. He talked a great deal about a great many things, and Rider said yes, yes, he understood, all the while nodding and not looking away while Dido transported over into the looming vessel directly onto the flight deck of the shuttlecraft to question and powered it up and took off and headed back in tandem with Rider out of the Border Zone and back toward the *Enterprise* patiently waiting like a thing extant before the expanding universe itself had burst into being, and the Merengi, still speaking of the importance of shiny buttons and hygiene and shuttlecraft etiquette and the metaphysical and existential matters with which all illiterate and uneducated peasants are preoccupied, never noticed until they had gone and left behind them only the unpleasant odor all humans left in the noses of Merengi.

Rider and Dido gave the shuttlecraft their head and ran them till their warp cores were lathered and frothing, and they let go the navigation controls because given free rein a shuttlecraft will always find its own way home.

Willie Rider in his faithful *Scout* contacted Dido on the recovered *Rosinante* and congratulated him on a job well done.

Oh, shucks, Commander. It were not nothing.

Rider frowned. In the background he could hear music. What's that you're playing, Mr Dido?

Aaron Copland, Commander. It seemed appropriate, somehow.

LADY FED

Not by

Jackie Collins

Demanda Trois was svelte and dark-eyed, the kind of woman whose every move said "I know what I want and I know how to get it." She had grown up among the wealthy and titled on her native Betacam, and she was used to being surrounded by luxury. She had owned holofilm-production studios and resort-casino asteroids, and she had made and traded fortunes the way children swapped grav-ball cards. But as much as Demanda had owned, she had never been owned, not by any man. And she never would be. She was young and independent and rich and free, and she was beautiful and powerful. Bearing these burdens was terribly lonely and painful for her.

When Demanda decided to enlist in Starfleet and serve on a Federation starship, her mother was shocked. "You can't live among those common people," Lwaxana declared. Lwaxana Trois had once been married to a paramount deity, and for a time had borne the title Mrs. Great Bird of the Galaxy. "You'll want out within six months, and I'll have to sleep with half of Starfleet Command to get you discharged. With honors, of course."

"You've already slept with half of Starfleet Command, Mother," Demanda retorted. "And when I come back, it will be in style."

Little did Lwaxana know how right her daughter was. But it wouldn't hurt to use her many industry connections to help Demanda out. . . .

I. Will Raker was known throughout the galaxy for the conspicuous gleam in his eye and the even more conspicuous bulge in his tight trousers. In his early thirties, his dashing good looks and Away Team exploits had given him a taste for adventure and exotic alien sex. "You've got a woman in every port," jealous and lesser men often accused. Raker twinkled and replied, "No, every woman *has* a port. I just dock there. And I *always* pull out on time."

Raker was First Officer aboard the star vehicle *Enterprise*, a glamorous and luxurious cruise ship that generated a billion credits a year for the company that produced her. The *Enterprise* visited a different star every week. Last week it had been Madonna. Next week was the Bob Hopes, or maybe the Sidney Poitiers. The ship was affectionately nicknamed "the *Franchise*" by those who profited from her entertaining journeys.

Raker still had a spring in his step as he left sickbay after his semiannual proctological exam. Dr. Beverly Hills-Crusher had cheerfully probed him the old-fashioned way, and Raker had been happy to return the favor. Hills-Crusher was a natural redhead. Raker often boasted in the Ten-Polo Lounge that he had verified this himself. Beverly also had ultra-long dancer's legs and terrific tits which, being a doctor, she had installed herself. She often boasted of being a self-made woman.

Raker strode confidently around a corner in the corridor and stopped in his tracks.

"Demanda!" he exclaimed in surprise.

"Will! I just beamed on board."

They had had an affair once, long ago, when he had been married to a Bellairean countess for her money and Starfleet connections and Demanda had been seriously bound to—and sometimes by—Wyatt Miller, the Federation's most powerful producer of popular teen holodramas such as *Melrose Space*, *Sickbaywatch*, and *Landing Party of Five*. Demanda and Will's lovemaking had been hot as the Vulcan desert they'd fled to, but he had needed his space, and so their careers had put light years between them. Now Raker's eyes roamed across Demanda's skintight outfit like greedy hands. "You're on the *Enterprise* now?" he asked incredulously.

Demanda's eyes flickered with amusement. "Now and forever," she breathed huskily. "But I don't get on duty for another four hours."

Raker twinkled and stood more erect. "I don't care when you get on," he said indifferently. "I want to know when you get off. I already know how."

Demanda give him her cabin number: Deck 9, Cabin 0210. . . .

Captain Splichard turned from the image of Trois and Raker on the comm screen in his tastefully appointed Denebish Moderne ready room. So, Number One and the new ship's counselor had a history, eh? Well, that was good to know. It might come in handy. . . .

Chef-Cook Splichard was the only bald man ever to be named one of *Space-Time* magazine's "world's sexiest men." It was his voice that did it. When he spoke, women went home and wrung out their Calvin Klein pantyhose. Splichard had made it his business to know everything his crewmen did. He did it by spying on them. The ship's computer would show him anyone he asked for, anywhere they were. Their privacy was always subject to command override. His days of getting the goods on cross-dressing officers were long behind him, now that Starfleet had adopted a unisex uniform, but over his long and ruthlessly ambitious Starfleet career he had amassed a small fortune by blackmailing officers. Those credits were now gathering interest in unnumbered accounts in Ferengi banks.

The captain turned off the monitor. The idea of watching Raker drive that Betacam tramp with his impulse thruster was boring. The captain had just watched his Number One slipping his own number one to the good doctor. But Splichard was in no position to do anything about the good doctor's many dreary flings all over the ship, because the ball-busting bitch also knew the truth about the *Enterprise*'s virile captain. . . .

"Well, Giorgio, our time is up for today." Demanda stood up and patted Lt. Commander Giorgio La Forger's naked thigh. La Forger was sprawled like a panther on the real

Rigalian ox-leather Gucci couch in Demanda's quarters. He was a handsome young man who had climbed from humble roots until he could fix any machine. It was La Forger who maintained the ship's upscale Rodayo drive and ensured that the platinum charge cards stayed below their limits. Well, Demanda thought, this time someone worked on *his* Jefferies tube.

"Wow, thanks, Demanda," Giorgio said gratefully. "You've been a big help."

She smiled. "We'll explore this further tomorrow," she said coyly.

After Giorgio had gone and she had watched his tight little ass gliding down the corridor, Demanda called up her personal log and began dictating. Demanda was a great dictator, especially to personal logs. In the heat of passion, the engineer had called out a name, and that information might prove useful. She wondered, though, who "Wesley" might be. . . .

A coded subspace transmission arrived for Demanda just before she left to attend the lavish welcome-aboard party being thrown in her honor. It was from her mother on Betacam. Demanda read it and smiled with evil mean wickedness. Mother had come through. Demanda had known she would.

The party was held in the Ten-Polo Lounge. It was a stellar event. Demanda arrived at her party wearing a revealing silk gown spun by sentient caterpillars on Gneeman Markup III. This afternoon, she'd had her hair done by José the Eberian. Now Beverly Hills-Crusher glided over to her, sipping a glowing blue concoction and wearing an insincere smile above a dress Demanda privately thought she must have picked up in some discount boutique on the bad side of the Möbius Strip. "Demanda, darling, you look literally radiant!" The doctor kissed both cheeks in stylish warp-setter fashion. "I haven't seen one of those dresses in years!"

Demanda kept her smile on her face. Behind Beverly, Raker was looking at both of them. He toasted them, eyes twinkling. "I believe we have something in common, Beverly," Demanda said with catty irony.

Beverly glanced back at Raker. "Why, yes, I think we do. Stop by sickbay tomorrow, darling, and I'll give you an antibiotic for it."

Later on, Demanda was standing near the observation window when a voice spoke from the shadows. "I don't believe we've been introduced yet, Counselor," it said in deep, masculine tones of command. From an alcove stepped a short, bald man with a commanding bearing and ruthless ambition in his steely eyes. He was wearing a dress blouse from Armann-E, an insignia carved out of a combination of rare holly wood from the Universal City of Lost Angels and dense brent wood from the defunct colony of New Voreesh, and a formal kilt from Tartan I, a relic of the ancient and passé Kamali Empire. "Captain Splichard," he announced.

She coldly shook his hand. "Captain," she acknowledged. "I've been looking forward to . . . meeting you." She paused just long enough to imply worlds of meaning.

His lips smiled faintly. "We're very much alike, you and I," he said. "In another life we might have been friends." He bent closer to her to whisper. "Don't think I don't know what you've been up to."

Her black eyes blazing, Demanda started to demand an explanation. But just then Beverly Hills-Crusher staggered by, embarrassingly drunk as she always became whenever she hit the synthehol. "Talkin' to our cap'n, eh?" she slurred. "Well, don' bother to get him inna sack, shweetie." She put an arm on Demanda's shoulder. Demanda resisted an urge to slap it away. "Our fearless leader here has got a command problem, if you know what I mean." Her voice had gone drunkenly high, and all across the lounge uniformed personnel stopped swapping business cards and talking about the other roles they hoped to land after this vehicle had finished its run.

Splichard stepped forward with murder in his cold eyes. "Beverly—"

The doctor laughed meanly. "You may have a landing bay, honey, but he's got no shuttle."

"I won't have this aboard my ship." His tone was deadly. "Go to your cabin."

Demanda felt that now was the time to make her move. "*Your* ship?" she asked innocently. Her dark eyes blazed. "That's where you're wrong, *Mr.* Splichard. This is *my* ship now. Starfleet has decommissioned her and sold her as surplus to the High Mogul of Betacam—who just happens to be my mother." There was a gasp across the Ten-Polo Lounge. This was the moment Demanda had waited for, and she gloried in it. "Set a course for Betacam. I'm taking my ship home."

Beverly Hills-Crusher married the ex-president of the infamous Tri-Star Settlement and retired to private practice on the Malib-U Colony. She specialized in Vulcan and Romulan ear jobs and discreet forehead reductions for Klingon celebrities.

Giorgio La Forger was dishonorably discharged from the Federation for contributing to the delinquency of a minor. He is now a centrifuge repairman on the planet Maytag.

When I. Will Raker turned fifty, he tried to pick up a young woman in a bar on the Yup E outpost on Trader VIX. She laughed at him and called him a "dirty old man." Raker returned to his private yacht *Priapic,* set the transporter coordinates for maximum dispersion, and sent himself abroad.

Chef-Cook Splichard never recovered from losing his command. He became a syntheholic, and during an unsuccessful stint as a stand-up comedian on the Klingon homeworld of Khamali, he was mobbed after saying *Take my life—please!*

Authorities found him backstage, hanging from a rafter by his own intestines. He had been hoisted by his own petard.

Demanda Trois kept the *Enterprise* long enough to throw a fabulous party on board. There she met a fabulously wealthy and ruthlessly ambitious producer from 25th Century Fox with an enormous trouser bulge who cast her in his most expensive production ever. It flopped.

The *Enterprise* is now the *Shatner,* a privately owned, low-gravity geriatric hospital for retired thespians.

A Portrait of
the Artist
as a Young Fan

Not by

James Joyce

tately, bald, Captain Picarus came from the turbolift, bearing a personal log on which a cup of Earl Grey lay steeping. Solemnly he faced about the bridge and blessed gravely thrice his crew. On the viewscreen hurtled stars. *Imax sensurroundium.* You can almost hear them whizzing by. Billions and billions, Sagan said. Beautiful shitblack space.

He turned abruptly his great commanding eyes from the cosmos to an impassive corpsewhite face.

—Position, Mr Datalus?

—Orbiting Omphalos in twenty minutes, sir.

—Excellent. Wharf, you discommendated Klingon, convey my regards to the Agenbite of Inwit, and tell him we look forward to his reception this evening.

The Klingon, Moorish dark and convolute of brow, bent to do as he was told. Wharf, absurd moniker. My *cha'Dich,* the bladed *bat-leth* in his outthrust arms. Odor of traitors all him assailed. Dishonored family, but still. What's in a name, yes? *Worf-worf!* Down, boy! Poor dogsbody. And a pisspoor marksman to boot. How many times have I been whisked away on his watch?

—Mr Datalus, I'll be in my ready room.

—Aye, captain.

Cat-eyed Datalus. Bit of a golem, really. Have they souls, I wonder. Abomination if they don't. Still, no chance of eternal perdition if sinner be. Before the replicator he replenished his Earl Grey and ordered a nice fried kidney as well. The tea was strong and the captain said as much.

—When I makes tea I makes tea, the computer replied. And when I makes water I makes water.

Through the window the tragicosmos spitting stars. AF I carved into the elm tree at the Academy. Twenty-seven was it I graduated. How time flies. How I fly. Picarus father of Datalus spreads his thespian wings and waxes on. Flordie's engines hum a chant. *Ohmmmm*-phalos.

Ineluctable modality of the engine core—two hours to repair, if no more, estimated through my louvered eyes. Trim the dials of the dilithium. My eyes. Yet all outside me look on my body before them coloured. But enhanced I shut my eyes and see. Irrelevance of colour in my sight of circuitry: blueglow, snotgreen, shitblack. In the land of the two-eyed, the visored man is king. Or at least a vizier? Aye, so linear!

Flordie O'George closed his eyes to hear his shoefalls softly on the engineering deck. Short strides at warp speed. *Mobilis in mobilii.* Nemo's slogan, that. Five, six, now at *der warpenchamber.* Needless eyes: ineluctable modality of the visor. Check ship's course: en route Omphalos, aleph alpha mark nought nought one.

Warp core thrumming. *Lux eterna.* In the depths of my vessel I conjure fire like the Vulcan: *la forge, quelle blazes!* Fresh from the Academy I remember. You were going to engineer wonders, what? That womansbody on the holodeck, not flesh but light projected. Dr. Leah Brahms, was it. Strongwilled, soft rope of her hair. Noon watch, engine running smooth. Ah, a subordinate. See: he approaches. Sign his report. Bleep bloop blop. Good day, good day. *Exeunt omnias,* stage right.

His feet marched in proud rhythm along by the warp core. Hellsmouth there: annihilating matter. Meet me Auntie Mater. Well, which is she, damn your eyes?

Pax!

That time on the *Araby* lost among asteroids. Wandering rocks.

No one about. Think I'll pick my nose and wipe it 'neath the console.

Mr Datalus watched with relish the inner workings of machines. Sweets for the sweet. Wandering about the dou-blin' decks he grew concerned for his own inner being. He felt certain some software softness, ghost in his machine, was causing the incremental fragmentation of his faculties. Odour of wet ashes, false data.

In the corridor crewmates bustled. Occasional nods a kind of acronym: ICU. Felt his rear pocket for the letter. Damn: no pockets on these things. Cordially invited to attend. Informal reception. Agenbite of Inwit keynote speaker. Gray horror sears my flesh. Counselor Toil there. Wonder if it's true her and Buck Riker.

—Ah, Chief O'Brien. Top of the morning to you. How is the Mrs, and how is little Molly blooming? Fine, fine, good day to you too.

Him staggering from TenForward. Like someone's stolen his lucky charms. And it not even noontide. Hearts, moons, stars, clovers. Wonder how it is they think with all those feelings mucking them about. Walking bags of warm jelly. Not for me.

> I got no glands
> To hold me down
> I got no glands on me!

Clinking clanking collection of collagenous junk. Maybe activate my journalism program. See the world in header type, *Times* roamin'. How glandular we are this morning.

IN THE HEART OF THE
HYPERSPATIAL METROPOLIS

Ah, yes, the reception. The Agenbite of Inwit, beamed motelike from Omphalos. Attend thee his brothers, aye. Initiate smalltalk subroutine A-3.

FALSE DATA

Another canapé, Herr Ambassador? Lemon platt, butterscotch? Oh, I daresay: stuffed to bursting with sweetstickies, eh? Ha! Must build up your reserves for the conference on Gaylik II, what? And have you met our good doctor here? Hair of Erin and a bedside mannerist. Talk, talk amongst yourselves! Ask him, good Doctor, how exactly one becomes such an Agenbite. I depart to greet Ensign Ellison.

Kerry Ellison!

so and here it is stardate six sixteen point one-two and Ill bet hes good and sauced at the 10Forward him and his stretchuniformed cronies officer material he told me so I replied they look like jammies to me still I like a man in uniform I liked him upon a once so to kiss his bald head O wretched Datalus whiteglancing speculative from me to Buck Riker at that interminable reception for that nitwit or whatever he was an endless train of canapes have taken from me the girlish figure of my youth so I hiked my skirt naughtily and gave him a taste of why they call me crusher in the first place wretched Database but O captain my captain when on shore leave you and I went away alone at last along the riverrun on Algeciras VII with its little pale natives white dwarves you called them the white dwarf sun shines for you he said that day we lay among the stunflowers when I got him to proposition me leading him on with that ferengi aphrodisiac I hypoed him with so I could ask him with my ayes would he so I was thinking of so many previous episodes Tashas flatline on the biobed and that quarky ferengi on DS 9 with the back-facing veil halfround his potatohead asking me to step into his little bit of a ship the Fitzromulans and the McCardassians and the O'Vulcans and who knows who else from the Federation and all ends of the Alpha Quadrant and Wes away alas along the Academy and so that poor Kaelonian Timicin euthanizing at sixty Timicide youd have to call it can you imagine poor Lwaxana Toil and all her Betazed tears the towers of starbase vi and baccarat on deepspace nine and the night we missed the shuttle on algeciras vii o the cosmos shitblack sometimes and the enterprise where im a doctor of the federation so how i hypoed my captain so and asked him so would he make it with me so and he said yes hed make it he would so make it doctor make it so

The Vampire
Le Forge

Not by
Anne Rice

I can't see . . . " said the engineer thoughtfully, and slowly he walked across the engine room toward the bow. For a long time he stood there against the hurtling lights and the passing specks of matter. "Not the way you think of seeing, anyway," he said at last. "For me the spectrum includes lush infrareds and prose-purple ultraviolets. I see residual heat and I see. . . . " He stopped for a moment, then turned and looked at the young man with a private smile.

"Energy," he finished.

He gestured with an elegant hand at the tricorder on the table. "Is that on?" he asked. "I want to tell my whole story. . . ."

"I am the vampire Le Forge. My hair is black, tightly curled and close-cropped. My manner is highly affected, as is my speech. My skin is a smooth, even chocolate. My uniform is black and mustard yellow. My eyes—when you can see them—are blank white balls. If these colors don't look right to you, perhaps you need a visor as well.

"My visor. It's an acronym, you know: Vampiric Intake for Sensory Organ Replenishment. It has made me the creature you see before you. I didn't always wear it. Two hundred years ago I was completely blind. Congenitally blind, born without optic nerves. A liability to both my estranged parents (Mother a Starfleet command officer, Father an exo-zoologist), I was foisted off on either as their respective temperaments could withstand me, and shunted from parent to parent and planet to planet according to the dictates of their whims and careers. It would be nice to say I saw half the Federation while still a boy, but back then I saw nothing at all.

"When still a strapping young man I emigrated to New New Orleans under the Indentured Servitude Act. What I arrived at was slavery, plain and simple.

"Do you know the planet? The streets are always wet, it's muggy as a Tennessee Williams play, and the lighting is always purple.

"For years I toiled under the lash on Master Armand's paracotton plantation. I grew to anticipate with keen sharp pleasure the sting of the phaser whip across my naked sweating back. Eventually they had to separate the young and strong men from the others to work in the duranium mines. You don't need to see to shuck paracotton, but you do to mine duranium, an irony I always appreciated, for the mines were dark, and consequently I was provided with my visor. Even more ironic, I became an overseer.

"Conditions in the mine were gruesome and before long Armand found us revolting. We overran the estate, and as I rampaged through the power plant of the plantation an odd thing happened: the lights dimmed and the life-support systems weakened. Machinery ground to a halt. Yet as it happened, I grew stronger! My blood surged in my veins and I heard the songs of the ancients in my cells. How pathetically inadequate my strung-together adjectives are to describe it! I knew who was the walrus, and who buried Paul. I knew why the caged bird sang, and the lost language of cranes, and how many licks it took to get to the Tootsie Roll center of a Tootsie Pop. Nothing was denied me.

"Examining the power plant I discovered the corroded state of the diethylamide crystals, but I did not make the connection between their decayed state and my empowered one until I actually touched them. They decayed under my fingertips, while I—I grew stronger! I knew then that I was indeed a vampire, but a vampire of a different orientation. Not mere blood was my sustenance, but energy. Energy! My visor absorbed it and gave me strength. For energy is the blood of machines, and I myself am part machine—not just because of my visor, but in deportment as well.

"After the Federation had liberated New New Orleans, I contrived to keep my nature a secret, fearing the Starfleet Medical Academy's gruesome experiments. Instead I enlisted in the Academy itself and studied engineering. I did so because it put me in touch with the source of my need: diethylamide! How the very envelope of my skin sings at the mention of the word!

"My first assignment was to the *Victory,* and I served her faithfully and well, and drained her of every millijoule she could produce. It did not take long for my appetites to grow larger and more exotic, and I requested a transfer to a Galaxy-class vessel.

"I was promoted and assigned to the starship *Enterprise*, and before long I had acquired a reputation as a master mechanic and engineer. Whatever went wrong, through sheer ingenuity and dauntless determination I fixed it. The fools! They never suspected that I—*I!*—was the very source of their problems. Mysterious power drainages in the containment fields, fluctuations in the warp core, fluttering in the inertial dampers—I was the source of them all! For me to serve on the *Enterprise* was like unto the traditional type of vampire driving a bloodmobile. Really, can you imagine a starship having such fundamental power problems on a steady basis? It buggers—er, beggars—the imagination. But rather than suspecting me as their problems' source, I was hailed as a savior for solving them.

"After I had made a steady diet of the vessel and had my way with any number of power sources, I began to believe that Lieutenant Commander Beta suspected me. I had long regarded him enviously and felt his magnetic attraction. We worked together constantly, and his unemotional, wooden presence made me feel more akin to him than any other crew member. My only other friend during this whole time was a Borg named Hugh—also a machine. I consumed him and converted him into a creature such as myself, and then I sent him back to his own kind. The Borg were finished two years later. Poor Hugh simply had no self restraint.

"At any rate, I thought to nip Beta's suspicions in the bud and one day told him flat-out I would like to have him for dinner in my cabin. I fed him a succulent fettucine with pumpkincréme sauce, along with fava beans and an excellent chianti. I knew Beta did not need to eat, but I wished to tantalize his palate before I whetted mine. I admired his pale, unblemished skin and cataracted eyes, the graceful economy in the movements of his engineered hands. Beta had much energy in him, and my plan was to have him, to take him into me and drain him and leave the crew with a spent member.

"By dinner's end I had maneuvered my mechanical prey onto the edge of my bed, telling him I had some interesting new human things to show him, for he was always willing to go where no man has gone before. It was in expectation of exploring such strange new worlds that he tilted his pale face up to me when I told him to look into my visor. I concentrated on sucking the abundant energy from him, leaving him empty and me strong—when to my astonishment I discovered that *I* was the one being sucked dry! There was a warm smell of calitas rising up in the air; my head grew heavy and my sight grew dim; and it seemed I heard an eagle singing. I felt a distant pressure and realized it was Beta gripping my shoulders. 'I'm dying,' I shouted. 'Dying.' I tore away from him and gradually my sight returned. 'You!' I accused. 'You are . . . like me!'

"'More so,' he replied. 'For I could suck the charge off a photon torpedo. I am a machine, Le Forge, and draining energy is my nature. You are raw and untrained. Oh, you are mechanistic enough for the rest of these crew members, but you must become more like a machine. You must be taught.'

"From then on we were constant companions and con-federates in crime. Naturally, I overheard the veiled com-ments in Ten-Forward, but I was unconcerned. My lust was for power. Beta was my teacher, my mentor, and an ever-ready energizer. He confided to me that he had been born an energy vampire, the creation of Soong the Oldy Moldy One. In retrospect Beta's existence as a vampire should have been obvious to me from the start—he was undead, he had inhumanly fast reflexes, he did not age and would live forever, he did not sleep, he could directly access the computer and the ship's energy conduits, he possessed great strength, his skin was pale, and his eyes were feline. Most damningly, he never once tugged his uniform top to keep it in place. He was a supernatural being, all right, a vampire operating not covertly but in broad—you'll forgive the allusion—daylight.

"My own skin? Oh, but it has paled considerably since my boyhood; I was once much darker than what you now see. And my eyes, well—they are as odd as Beta's were.

"Beta taught me how to drain the energy from a scene so thoroughly and subtly that even in the midst of a Red Alert facing a Globulan warbird, everyone on the bridge acted with an astonishing listlessness, a lethargic rote-like func-tioning that made them all seem as performing mannequins.

"All, that is, but Captain Jacquard. He declaimed and vituperated in a manner that seemed even more exagger-ated against the sluggish wanness of the bridge crew. I asked Beta about it once and he merely replied, 'I suspect the captain is impervious to our best efforts. Some people simply cannot be . . . repressed.'

"There is really very little left to tell. The biography of one such as myself is bound to be somewhat bereft of plot. What counts is the baroqueness of prose and details of dress, cuisine, architecture, and *faux* French *poseur* sensibility. With a healthy dollop of *double-entendre* homoeroticism for those of confused orientation, naturally. Besides, were I to tell you the entire tale, what profit could I reap from future installments?

"But I note that your tricorder is no longer functioning and that you, yourself, seem to be fading fast. I can only surmise that listening to a tale such as mine, and even the effort to remain absorbed by such an artificial and contrived atmosphere of gothic aspiration, is nothing less than . . . draining."

Even Captains Get the Blues

Not by
Tom Robbins

Napoleon said, "A man should be measured from his head to the sky." Naturally, Napoleon's head was a bit farther from the sky than most people's. Which is why, in history's greatest recorded case of over-compensation, he went and conquered most of the Western world. It was Napoleon who blew the Sphinx's nose. He used a cannon. If only he had heard of elevator shoes.

In any case, you must be at least THIS tall to read this episode.

Beaver Le Crusher tossed her tomato-colored tresses as her phthalo-blue eyes sponged up the schwoopy set of parabolas gliding toward her down the corridor: hips like parentheses bracketing a steamy sentence in Henry Miller. Breasts whose curvature would make Federation police read Miranda rights to a stoic Vulcan heart, informing it that it was under cardiac arrest.

The curvy apparition stopped when she saw Le Crusher. Her dewy doe-ey gaze sent uncoded subspace transmissions. She drew a phaser from a holster around her tie-dyed Dedahed dress and twirled it expertly. "Well, howdy, pardner," she called in an accent like an Israeli taught English by a Texan living in London. "You must be the new doc. Shoot, no one tole me you was a carrot top."

"Beaver Le Crusher." Le Crusher held out a hand.

The Dedahed accepted it like she was licking it with her fingers. "Welcome aboard the *Enterprise* Ranch, Crush. NCC-1701 dash LSD. Heck, I'm a doc myself. Menaja Trois, at your cervix."

"Anyone ever tell you you were schwoopy?" Le Crusher asked.

"Heck, no. I don't even know what it means."

"It's a Klingon word," Le Crusher explained as they walked arm-in-arm down the corridor. "It's an engineering term used to describe something designed without a ruler. If you pour water on something schwoopy, it all runs off. Sixty-nine Corvettes and Bettie Page are schwoopy."

"Shoot," said Trois. "So happens I got a hologram of Bettie Page doing sixty-nine in a Corvette on my cabin wall. Wanna see?"

In Trois' cabin she held Le Crusher's hand like a wounded dove. "I want you to give me a Level One diagnostic, Doc," she said. "I think my inertial fields are dampening." She moved the dove a little lower. "Ah," she said. And: "Oh." And: "Ooh," And sometimes: "Y."

The rangy redhead grinned and pushed her back onto the bed. "Yep, I'd say your shields were down and you were in danger of an imminent core breach."

Trois looked up with glazing eyes. "Maybe if you manipulated my plasma conduits," she breathed, "you could initiate a meltdown."

Le Crusher agreed. Then she proceeded to plunder the walls of Trois.

We would like to take this opportunity to nominate the official fruit of this episode. Because of its tenacious gift for prospering wherever it is sown—indeed, often where it is not wanted—and because of its ability to grow in thin air and back lots on a steady diet of mostly bullshit, yet still bear lucrative fruit, we would like to nominate the German red bush, or *rötenberry,* as the official fruit of this episode.

Uniforms back on and faces toweled dry, Le Crusher and Trois were part of the welcoming delegation when the ambassador from P'an beamed aboard. The P'an had evolved from a goat-like ancestor. The upright little devils came complete with brown fur, slit yellow pupils, cloven hooves, and horns, and they exuded a pheromone that had a peculiar and devastating effect on females all across the galaxy. Someone should bottle it.

The ambassador faded onto the platform like the Goat of Christmas Past. He looked like a stuffed-animal version of himself.

The effect was immediate. First Officer Biker and the Frog stood blinking, but Trois and Le Crusher rushed to the P'an and began fondling and petting him. "Ladies," barked the Frog, "this is hardly appropriate." But the men had already noticed—they couldn't avoid noticing it, really—the huge, throbbing, eggplant-colored erection poking from the P'an. The ambassador was a living coat rack.

The ambassador was sequestered in his quarters and women were forbidden access to him. Trois immediately went to the captain's randy room to confront the Frog.

The Frog's real name was Lon-Jacque Tankard. He'd been raised in a vineyard by Zen French isolationists whose only source of entertainment had been the plays of Shakespeare. The Frog was bald as an egg's behind and horny as a bull parade. Trois found him seated in lotus position in his ratty white bathrobe with its incongruous monogrammed comm insignia, consulting his laptop Ouija board and sipping his customary Payeaux tea. Behind him was a globular aquarium in which colorful Magic Rocks were growing.

"Hello, Counselor," said the Frog. "You're looking very paisley today."

Trois set a hand near her trusty phaser and schwooped to conquer. "The female members of the crew resent your repressive patriarchal bourgeois Christian domination. We've taken over the Engineering Section, and we demand the release of that cute li'l goat fella. And from now on the replicators can serve only brown rice, mushrooms, and beans and franks."

She left abruptly as a backseat hump with Uma Thurman. Wow, thought the Frog as she schwooped on out of the randy room, her phaser sure is set on "stunning."

It is time to deliver the sad news that special-interest planets are lobbying to halt this episode in midwarp. These worlds manufacture allegedly hygienic products designed to coerce human women into believing that there is something unnatural about their leg hair, the natural mushroomy odor of their vaginas, and their glandular pheromones. These planets have expressed concern over what they consider to be this episode's advocacy of satanism. These are the same people who were afraid of the Procter & Gamble "man in the moon" logo, and they have failed to discern that pagans and Pan have nothing at all to do with Satan. Why worshiping the devil would make Christians fraidy cats anyhow is a mystery, since to revere Satan you have to believe in the Bible.

In any case, these planets have pulled their advertising from this episode, which is why you are able to read it with no further commercial interruptions.

You're welcome.

In the Engine Room the women come and go, talking of Mike and Angelo. Ensign Nada wanted to celebrate their antipatriarchal victory by taking medication that would make all the women menstruate at the same time, but everly loverly Beaver Le Crusher called the idea bloody ridiculous. "Let's don't burn our chickens before they're crossed," she warned.

"She's right," agreed Trois. "If we hatch our bridges behind us, we're dern tootin' gonna be outfoxed by them penis-wielding varmints."

Irish Lieutenant Sill O'Cybin frowned. "What about rescuing the P'an ambassador from his cabin? He's probably nibbled up everything in sight by now."

All the rebelling crewhands agreed, and a rescue mission was, like Jane Mansfield's infamous physique, mounted.

Half asleep in his pajamas, the Frog contemplated his naval training. He summoned Lieutenant Commander Dada and asked him about the situation. Dada was one of the Clock People, an assemblage of wires and gears and tape and the white paste you ate in elementary school that leads to heroin. Dada was in charge of the ship's chronometers, and he could alter the flow of time easy as winding a watch.

Being a Clock Person also meant Dada had no gender. He was burdened with neither testosterone nor estrogen, attended neither sporting events nor *kaffeeklatsches*. He was the perfect mediator for this situation.

Dada felt that there was nothing more natural than men and women together, except perhaps women and women together. For some reason he avoided altogether the issue of men and men together. He also felt natural redheads to be holy, and wondered if this might be because the author of his being also happened to be a natural redhead. Dada's solution to the rebellion was to take the P'an ambassador to sickbay and have him temporarily de-scented. Then he direct-beamed the P'an to the Engine Room, where he sparkled like an oncoming rush of ecstasy in the midst of the rebelatrixes. The reaction was just like when French pussycats realize Pepé Le Pew is a skunk: their cute corn-chip noses wrinkle and their doe-like eyes go wide as saucers before a melée in a Greek restaurant. "My god," screeched Beaver Le Crusher, "he's a goat! A stinky old *goat!*"

Menaja Trois fast-drew her phaser and created an inter-stellar incident.

Q Clearance

Not by
Tom Clancy

The bridge crew snapped to attention when Captain Petard emerged from his ready room wearing a puzzled frown. Ever sensitive to his superior's needs and moods, First Officer Striker rose from his chair, where he had been field-stripping his phaser, and tugged smartly on the hem of his uniform top. "Something wrong, Captain?"

Petard held up his arm. "My watch," he answered. "It seems to have stopped."

"Yellow Alert," Striker ordered. The bridge became an instant bustle of cool, efficient, and professional motion. At the Op Center, Lieutenant Commander Doodad, an autonomous Starfleet device often used to combat interstellar terrorists, immediately called up schematics of wrist chronometers with his left hand, while his right hand notified ADT, the Artifact Diagnostic Team on constant alert in the Engineering Section. Lieutenant Smurf narrowed the focus of the sensors at his Tactical station to determine whether the malfunctioning chronometer might be a source of explosive or radioactive hazard, and because he was a disciplined Starfleet officer as well as a Klingon and therefore a realistically paranoid warrior sensitive to any possibility of threat, he also tapped into the forward Ops station to determine whether any type of transmission might be emanating from the chronometer. Smurf had been born and bred a soldier, and he knew the pride that came from wearing a uniform, any uniform, Klingon or Starfleet or Postal Service, it didn't matter. So long as you had superiors and subordinates and got to carry a sidearm and guard things and learn codes and call out "Who goes there!" Smurf felt pity and contempt for those who had not experienced this privilege, and brotherhood toward those who did. Security was his business, and business was good.

Seated calmly at her own station to the left of the command chair, Counselor Meander Droid used her highly classified empathic abilities to glean any intent from the stopped watch, but all she could sense was a certain timelessness.

First Off Striker touched his ultra-high-tech, microminiaturized personal voice communications device, commonly known as a comm insignia. This pinnacle of Federation science had a range of nearly sixty thousand kilometers and could also be used as a location device and identifier, since it was equipped with dermal-sensor technology. It was so smart and context-sensitive that it knew when you wanted to talk even if you didn't touch it. It also knew who you wanted to talk to, and who else could listen in, and it knew when you were done talking. It even disregarded *sotto voce* comments. It had been adapted for espionage from a modified design stolen from the heathen Comulans.

"Striker to Valley La Forge."

"La Forge here."

"Report to the bridge. We have a problem."

"On my way."

Doodad approached Captain Petard and extended a melanin-deficient hand. "If I may, sir . . . ?"

Wordlessly the captain handed over his watch. The android held it up to his ear. "I detect no auditory metronomic indications of operation."

The captain looked exasperated. "Yes, Mr. Doodad, it's stopped ticking."

By the time Doodad had unscrewed the back of the watch, Valley La Forge stepped from the turbolift with his tool kit in hand. Petard's pacemakered heart swelled with an old soldier's pride as he watched La Forge and Doodad work efficiently as a single field-hardened unit dedicated to preserving the ideals and principles represented by the Federation and its technology, even down to the level of its commanding officer's chronometers.

"The dilithium-crystal movement seems to be regular," Doodad observed.

La Forge nodded. "Energy feed from the power couplings tests positive. Let's try rerouting auxiliary power from the mainspring to the inertial coil."

Doodad shook his head. "That will reduce temporal accuracy by thirty percent."

The engineer frowned. He regarded the watch through the ultra-fine-resolution lenses of his VISOR (Virtually Impenetrable Syntax for Organizing Republicans), a visual aid that doubled as a nightscope. "Doodad," he said, "let's take this baby down to Engineering and run a diagnostic."

Doodad looked puzzled. "This chronometer is in a natal stage, La Forge?" he asked.

"Never mind, Doodad. Let's go."

Down in Analysis Retention (ANAL RETENT) the watch was subjected to molecular analysis and found to be constructed of a tritanium/duranium alloy similar to the hull of the *Enterprise*. It could withstand any attack short of serious critical analysis. "It also has a nifty twist-o-flex band," said La Forge. He demonstrated.

"What won't they think of next," Doodad commented. He poured himself and La Forge a couple of Hennessys, neat. They drank the smoky liquor and reminisced about the primitive days of the Old Federation, when men were men and Klingons were scared, when captains fired first and opened hailing frequencies later. "No sense getting misty-eyed over the good old days," said La Forge, dabbing a camouflage handkerchief beneath his VISOR. "Let's brainstorm." The watch repair had already been code-named *Tempus Fuggit* and declared EYES ONLY, no offense to Mr. La Forge.

The crystal watch face was shatterproof metadiamond. In darkness the numerals glowed green with phosphene decay. "Look," said La Forge, holding it up from the microscan imager, "it also shows the phases of the moon."

"Which moon?" asked Doodad.

La Forge glared behind his VISOR and ignored him. "I still think it's an energy-source problem."

"It is possible," Doodad hypothesized, "that the captain's watch stopped because the *Enterprise* encountered a region of subspace interlaced with temporal rifts. Even a small one, if the captain's wrist passed through it, would be sufficient to cause temporal flux."

"Hmm." The engineer turned the watch in his hands. "What if," he began slowly, "there were a creature on board the ship that lived on pure energy, and it attached itself to the captain, sensing his command status. The broken watch might be proof that it was draining him like some kind of parasite."

The android nodded. "Or perhaps the watch itself is the creature," he mused.

"Or maybe the watch runs by using a pinhole singularity, like the Comulan warbirds, and somehow it's gone awry."

They looked at one another, the same idea forming in their respectively gelatinous and positronic brains. Immediately they rushed to the resonance imager and placed the watch under it. "Activate scan," said La Forge.

"There," said Doodad. "Coordinates four-four two mark two." The image on the screen shifted.

"Magnify," said La Forge. The image swelled.

"Gotcha," said La Forge.

Before them on the screen was a single brand name: ROMULEX.

From behind forcefield shielding Doodad worked on the watch with a pair of waldos. The mechanical grapples received data input from his own movements as transmitted by the computer. They had been invented in the primitive days of nuclear-fusion reactors.

Petard's authoritative voice came over the intercom. "Mr. Doodad, report."

"We have had our first break in the watch case, Captain."

"You *broke* it?"

"La Forge and I have devised yet another ingenious theory about the malfunction, sir. We think there may be minute quantities of matter and antimatter contained in quark-level containment fields in your watch case."

"Are you telling me it's a miniature warp core?"

"Similar, sir. Protons and antiprotons would be released at regular intervals, but if an imbalance forms—"

"Your watch would be off," La Forge finished.

"Mr. La Forge, if an imbalance forms, my watch will undergo a warp-core breach. Even at that level it would destroy the entire engineering hull."

"Which is why I am utilizing the waldos, Captain."

"Just don't get hiccups," said La Forge.

"Hiccups?" asked Doodad.

At that moment the lights dimmed and a figure dressed as legendary Earth deity General George S. Patton appeared.

"Q!" exclaimed La Forge.

Doodad stepped forward. "It is offensive for you to wear that uniform," he said. "You have not earned the distinction of military service. Remove it immediately or I shall terminate your life functions in a highly trained and patriotic manner."

"At ease, fellas." The omnipotent being with anarchist leanings saluted them with his riding crop. "What's all the ruckus?"

"Well," began La Forge, "The captain's—"

Q spied the watch on the diagnostic theatre. "Say, that's a handsome Romulex you've got there."

Doodad and La Forge gaped as Q blithely reached through the containment field and lifted the watch from the theatre. "And what seems to be wrong with the poor thing?" He stroked the watch and cooed at it.

"It is temporally deficient," said Doodad.

"I beg your pardon?"

"The captain's watch has stopped," explained La Forge.

"Ah." Q brightened. "And I suppose you've examined it with the most current and impressive batch of your pitifully primitive Federation technology."

"You could say that," La Forge said grudgingly. "We've tried everything, but we can't even identify the source of the problem."

Q clucked disdainfully. "Government money in action," he intoned. "That's the problem with you Feds—you're so indoctrinated with all this gee-whiz technology that you never think to look for the obvious."

"The obvious?" Doodad inquired.

Q sighed and placed his thumb and index finger on a small serrated cap at the end of a slender stem on the side of the watch case and began dialing it in a direction that can only be termed *clockwise*.

There was a faint ratcheting sound and the watch began to tick.

Q grinned disingenuously and handed the watch over to La Forge. "There you go, boys. Good as new. Bet she took a lickin', though."

MOBY TREK
(ABRIDGED)

Not by

Herman Melville

all me irresponsible. Some years ago—the stardate is unimportant now—the irresistible motivation of several outstanding warrants and the certainty of my impecunious nature, caused me to enlist upon a Federation starship, for just as some men hold the briny Sea in their hearts, I have empty Space in my head.

I thought to get myself aboard a vessel going a-holing, and went immediately for the most reeking pub I could find. Of the establishment itself I remember little, save that it was so populous with Klingoons I thought for a frightful moment I had happened upon a Kiss convention. After an unremembered repast of alcoholic splendor I awoke with a savage jerk. The jerk's name was Worf-worf (he being of the Klingoon persuasion), and whatever uncouth rituals we had enacted in the night, it turned out that on some worlds we were now legally married. He admitted he was a photoneer of no small experience and was himself seeking a hole-hunting ship, and that day we went to the space docks together to sign on.

[Omitted: 10,000 words describing the shuttle trip to the space dock.]

. . . at length we stood upon the wheelchair-inaccessible transporter platform of the *Enterprise,* a rare old craft of spindly design. She was a Galaxy-class ship of the old school, with giant mid-mounted twin nacelles standing stiffly like flying buttresses. If you ask me, she resembled nothing so much as a Dymo labeler.

Now looking about for someone in authority we saw a broadshouldered fellow with an arrogant posture, bearded in Quaker fashion and standing about importantly. We enquired if he were the captain, which seemed to amuse him greatly. "Captain Jean-Luc Piquod is the master o' this ship," he growled, "and ye'll see enough o' him iffin ye sign on. Ye've the honor of addressin' Billy 'Bud' Piker, Chief Mate. And who be you?"

"Call me Email," I said.

[Omitted: 8,000 words describing Worf-worf's and Email's qualifications.]

[Omitted: 5,000 words in which the crew contract is reproduced word for word.]

[Omitted: 10,000 words describing the name and occupation of each crew member, and the contents and shipping history of virtually every crate loaded on board for the expedition.]

We came to the sign of the Ten & Four, which was the emblem of an ancient harpoon head etched in glass upon pneumatic doors. Worf-worf's filed teeth and savage bearing earned us a table to ourselves, and barkeep Guinan Starbuck offered us coffee. Captain Piquod remained invisibly enshrined within his cabin and it was Chief Mate Piker who gave the order to depart space dock. We left Nuevo New England making two warps and singing old holing chanteys. Datta-goo,

2nd Harpooneer and innocent pale to Worf-worf's savage dark, lofted his mug and led a round:

There once was a ship called Nantucket,
Whose captain was heard to say—

"Feh!" yelled Worf-worf. "That no songee for a warrioree!" And he began an aria from one of his Klingoon *operas sauvage:*

There once was a pon farring Vulcan,
Who couldn't get near enough—

"Sure and it's that old one, is it?" shouted Irish C.P.O'Brien. "Lend an ear, fellas, an' I'll sing ya one about me favorite ensign!"

Ro, Ro, Ro, yer butt's
Gentle as a dream—

[Omitted: 127 additional space chanteys.]
Now, an interesting thing about the preference among hole hunters for Starbuck's coffees . . .
[Omitted: 5,000 words describing coffee varieties, grinds, blends, brewing, origins, methods of growth, and decorative ceramic drinking mugs.]
Some days elapsed, and asteroids all astern, when to the astonishment of all Captain Piquod summoned all hands into the shuttleboat bay. As we assembled he paced about

upright on deck, tugging nervously on his uniform top, bald pate gleaming. "What do ye do when sensors detect a black hole, men?" he cried. "Call out position!" we sang back. "And a white hole?"

Chief Datta-goo raised a hand blanched ever to a pallor of despair. "'Tis white holes we seek, sir?"

"Aye!" Piquod called back. "The white hole! That damnable pulsing quasar of the cosmic depths!" He pointed to his hairless pate. "'Twas such a one took off my hair, my hearties! We rammed, and were bombarded with neutrinos, and tidal forces tore the *Type A* apart, and overnight my hair grew white, and within a week had all fallen—prematurely—out. Yet I wear not a rug, nor a weave, as some lesser skippers have been known to do." He raised a fist. "Aye! The Great White Hole! I'll chase her 'round the Coal Sack and the Crab Nebula 'afore I give her up. That's what ye've signed on for, men!—We're bucking for an Emmy this mission! And whoso-ever calls out her position first will receive this!" He held out a beautifully wrought dagger, and beside me Worf-worf grunted his surprise. Piquod heard it. "I see thou recognizeth the ceremonial *Gin-soo* knife of thy savage forebears, my brave photoneer! It sliceth, it diceth, it maketh the julienne to fry!" He squinted at Worf-worf and theatrically raised an accusing finger. In a low voice he intoned, "I tell you again, Mr. Piker—I hate the Moor."

At mess that evening the dinner subject was indeed a singu-larity. The White Hole, mysterious source of emergent matter, spewing plumes of energy that may be from black holes, or from other dimensions entire. These strange spinning fish were first predicted well before spaceflight by those old space prophets Einstein and Rosen, who, according to their formulae. . . .

[Omitted: 10,000 words of black-hole and quasar physics.]

[Omitted: 5,000-word description of Worf-worf's and Dattagoo's photon harpoons, including the 100-verse rime that begins, "Pheeta, phoota, photoneer, Great White Holes will now appear!"]

[Omitted: A chapter on the whiteness of white holes.]

Now the fated *Enterprise* had been so long aspace the voyage, that soon the strobing geyser given forth by the Great White Hole was palpable to all the sensors.

"Thar she glows!" called I from my station. "Thar she glows!"

"Whar?" the captain demanded.

"Thar!"

"Heave ye hard about!" the captain ordered.

Deorkie La Fjörd looked up from his station. "Have I heard about what, sir?"

"Damn your eyes, turn the ship!"

Piker stood on the bucking quarterdeck. "Insult not his eyes, Captain, for he hath none!"

The captain nodded. "Those are pearls that were his eyes," he muttered. "Very well—Lower the warps', ahead half impulse! Ye there on the shuttleboats, look sharp! Helmsman May O'Naze, steady on our course—head us not within ye

Sheisskopf Radius, or ever Father Time will keep us guests! Drop anchor! Mr. Piker, launch boats! Mr. Parsec, arm photon harpoons! Look alive, me brave photoneers!"

Piquod faced the viewscreen and raised a fist. "Oh, enticing Hole! Thou shinest on and maketh me more Biblical by the word! My thespian heart is stir'd, my soliloquies yet unspoken!"

The boats were away, and Worf-worf sank a probe that transmitted until the White Hole dragged it under, and the *Enterprise* played about, riding the photon currents and gravitational tides the White Hole sent after us. The palpitations of the quasar strained us mightily, and soundings of the Red Alert rang greatly in our ears. The great creaking ship was sucked toward the hellish gravity well of the White Hole itself. Upon the viewscreen I saw first one then another shuttleboat stove in. In wretched cowardice I crawled the ratlines up the Jefferies tube and there with tricamcorder in trembling hand I watched the teledrama unfold. The bulkheads groaned as the tidal forces rended us asunder; with a wrench[1] the Saucer separated from the Engineering Section. On my screen I saw Piquod railing profoundly at the nemesis that filled his own screen. "Fie!" he declaimed. "Get thee to a nunnery! Not Montalban nor Shatner but *I* shall speechify at thee, foul quasar! Aye, very like a hole! Shine on, thou crazy diamond! Set the controls for the heart of the sun! Atom-heart mother! Astronomy

---

[1] *Wrench,* Amer. usage : in the United Kingdom, a *spanner.*

domine! But I suffer a momentary lapse of reason! In the history of the Cosmos thou and I art mere footnotes[2] yet on thee I would make my mark. On my mark—engage! Cold—I shiver—How now? Top of the world, Ma! Rosebud!"

And so saying, the ill-starred vessel was quartered in twain, and hurtled spinning, and in the last glimpse left to me I saw Piquod before the photon-torpedo controls with a hand on the firing button and a fist raised at the screen as into the maw he and all the saucer section plunged. "Toward thee I fall, thou all-destroying but unconvincing hole," he railed. "To the last fade-out I grapple with thee; from hyperbole's heart I act at thee; for King Lear's sake I vent my spleen at thee. Thou damn'd hole! *Thus* I give up my career!" And pressed he the firing button.

Now the White Hole spasmed in its stellar death throes, and gravitational tides seized the saucer, and all its crew, all round and round its vortex, and carried the smallest microchip of the *Enterprise* out of sight.

The melodrama's done, and I only am escaped alone by myself and no one else to tell thee singly, thy unknown messenger Email. Through hazardous and technically unexplainable physics, I evaded the vortex and was set adrift, until my beacon summoned to me the good freighter *Andre Andorian*. Call me finished and color me gone.

---

[2]The footnote has an interesting history itself, about which more anon.

THE TREKKING

Not by

Stephen King

Ready Room

Will Wriker thought: *officious little Pricard.*

The captain of the *Enterprise* sat across from him in the ready room. I am in charge, his upright posture said. When Wriker had come in, the bald man had continued fiddling importantly with a terminal screen whose face he kept turned away from view. Wriker was certain it was an electronic Etch-A-Sketch.

"I hope you understand what you're volunteering for, Will. The ship will be completely deserted. Life support will be minimal, not even functioning on some decks. We'll be on shore leave on a world that doesn't allow complex devices of any kind; you won't be able to contact us in an emergency. That kind of deprivation can get to a man."

Wriker smiled, a big wide subordinate smile. "Space fever? I'm not too worried about that. I'm looking forward to getting back to work on my womanizing memoirs."

Both men shared a beefy chuckle. "You're positive?" the captain persisted. "The last man who volunteered for solitary duty—well, some things are best left unsaid. Let's tour the ship, shall we?"

The Tour

All alcoholic beverages had been cleared from Ten-Forward. "But you'll be on constant duty," the captain said, "and won't need anything of that nature, eh?"

"Of course not,
(officious little)
sir."

"Fine." The turbolift brought them to the engine room.

"The engine core has been damped," Pricard explained. "But it isn't completely stable. The safeties are automated, of course, but there's a chance something might become . . . overlooked. If this gauge gets below Level Five, you'll have a warp-core breach on your hands."

"Understood, sir."

As they passed the holodecks on their tour, Wriker mentioned that he was looking forward to a little virtual reality R & R. "I expect you are, Mr. Wriker." A shadow crossed the captain's face. "Only . . . promise me you'll avoid Holodeck 217."

"Holodeck 217, sir? Is it malfunctioning?"

"You could say that." The captain frowned. "Yes, you could certainly say that."

Command Chair

Two weeks later Wriker sat in the captain's command chair, logging his memoirs. Around him the ship was empty and quiet and just a little spooky.

Let's see, there'd been those two Klingon women on the

Pagh; he'd hardly been able to stand next day. And that Bajoran woman with the unexpected ridges. Under twin moons they danced and drank

(oh wouldn't that be nice now a big tall cool one and maybe a drink too, heh-heh-heh)

Wriker snarled and snapped off the log. He did not notice the console blinking beside him. He wanted a drink, wanted a woman, wanted

(Dissecta)

to stop thinking about these things. Dissecta Troll was forbidden to him now. That shameful night after the poker game, he'd been drunk and she'd been on hands and knees picking up spilled chips

(liquor in front, poker in the rear!)

and he hadn't remembered much next day, and they never talked about it. He'd sworn off drinking and gambling and women and aliens and drugs and violence. Was it his father? Was he still trying to impress Kyle Wriker? Hadn't undergoing the *punzo-gai-roku* been enough to impress the old boozer? Is that why he had turned down offers to command the *Drake,* the *Aries,* and the *Melbourne?*

The console chimed, and now Wriker looked at it. According to the computer, the transporter was activating itself.

Ten-Forward

Ten-Forward was cold and lonely. Wriker sat at the bar and tried to control his shaking.

(it couldn't be him he's gone he joined the Maquis Sade he was captured by Hardassians, for christ sake)

(god I could use a—)

He stopped. In front of him was a sweating glass of pale yellow liquid. Wriker stared. He picked it up and drank deeply. Somulan pisswater. Yessiree, bub. Wriker toasted the empty bar. "*Salud,* boys. I've been away but now I'm back."

"Good evening, Mr. Wriker," said Trasha Yard in wooden tones. "It's good to see you." She stood behind the bar, lit unflatteringly from below. She didn't look at all well.

"Good to be seen, Trasha. Another round." Wriker polished off the ale and patted his uniform. "They don't make pockets on these damn things."

"On the house. Orders from the captain." She set another ale on the bar.

Wriker nodded and hefted the mug. "Funny thing happened to me on the way to the transporter room," he said.

"Really." Trasha's voice had no inflection.

"Yup." He drank. "The transporter turned itself on, and sure and begorrah there stood me own evil twin brother Thomas, right there on the platform. He never completely materialized; I could see right through him." Wriker leaned forward. "And you know what Tommy-boy did, Trasha?"

"What?" Her expression never changed. Come to think of it, it never had.

Wriker finished off his ale. "He raised his hand and pointed at me, and he said, 'Orkay Reach Bay.' Then he disappeared. You ever hear of a place called Orkay Reach Bay, Trasha?"

"Never."

Wriker shook his head. "You can't have two Number Ones on board. Can ya, Trash old girl?"

"You're Number One, sir. You've always been Number One."

Wriker frowned. "Say, Trasha . . . Weren't you killed on Vagra II? And then killed again by Somulans?"

Trasha's face remained blank. "I don't have any recollection of that at all, sir."

Wriker pushed away from the bar. "Ah, screw it. The way you acted when you were on this ship, I wasn't sure you were alive then, either. Thanks for the drinks." He saluted and left.

Holodeck 217

Wriker stood outside Holodeck 217. He was humming softly and tunelessly.

(You promised.)

(Orkay Reach Bay)

(I do believe in spooks, I do I do I do believe in spooks!)

(Uhh . . . Flight 666, you are cleared for takeoff, over)

The holodeck door opened without his command. Wriker gulped and went inside. The lighting changed as the computer sensed his presence, and vague shapes took form around him. Female shapes. Naked female shapes. They looked like holographic centerfolds. Holographic centerfolds of

(No, it couldn't be—)

of every woman Wriker had slept with. The room was filled with them. There were the two Klingon women from the *Pagh*. There was that redheaded pleasure girl from Risa. Ohmigod, there was Minuet, his favorite holodeck fantasy.

Wriker glanced back toward the door. It was shut. He looked back at the naked women and frowned. Something was different.

His breath stopped in his throat.

The naked holograms had changed position. That Malcorian woman now facing him, the one he'd slept with on a First contact mission

(Lanel her name was Lanel)

hadn't she been on her hands & knees a second ago? He put his hands over his eyes. *Oh, Willie-boy, two mugs of Somulan piss and you're—*

He lowered his hand. They were definitely closer. And they were all looking at him now. Wriker glanced back toward the door. Three women had edged toward it to block him off. They moved when he couldn't see them! He couldn't look at them all at once. There were hundreds, maybe thousands. The galaxy was big, after all, and he'd put in at a lot of ports

(heh-heh-heh)

"Where there's a Will, there's a way!"

Wriker gasped. Dissecta's voice! She stood before him now, naked and voluptuous. Wriker screamed and ran for the door, heard the women fumbling behind him as he slapped the wall plate and the door hissed open. Just as he bolted outside, it seemed he felt the rasp of a lacquered nail against the back of his uniform.

Orkay Reach Bay

The turbolifts were running by themselves, opening to admit invisible guests. An old flat-television theme by Alexander Courage gushed from the PA in every corridor. Laughter came from behind cabin doors. Decks without life support were lit and warm. Someone had ripped the condenser coils out of all the shuttlecraft and the transporters were leaking something that looked like blood. Human blood, the red kind. There was no escape. The engine room was—

Wriker stopped.

Engine room. The warp core. He pictured a gauge. *If this gets below Level 5. . . .*

Orkay Reach Bay. Igpay Atinlay.

Core Breach.

Wriker ran. The deck was covered in confetti and vibrated beneath his feet. The ship was powering up.

In the engine room he hurried past the warp core, which glowed a brilliant blue along its long tubular body. It was huffing and rattling and hissing off plumes of radioactive mist in a hundred directions like a Ferengi ocarina. The gauge stood at Level 1.

Thomas Wriker stood between Will and the warp-core jettison controls. *"Come join us, Willie boy!"* yelled William

Wriker's evil twin. *"Captain's orders!"* He grinned insanely. *"All work and no play gives boys a dull Will!"*

Wriker ran toward him. They collided and spun to the floor. Wriker pushed the doppelgänger away and put his hands on the warp-core jettison controls.

"Dad always liked you best!" screamed Thomas.

The shriek was swallowed in a matter/antimatter annihilation as the *Enterprise*'s warp core breached.

Shore Leave

Captain Pricard was fishing from the end of the holodock, forcing himself to enjoy his shore leave. His pole moved suddenly in his hand and he sat upright. His skull filled with light and the pole slipped from his lifeless hands. He shook his old bald head but could not clear away the thought that exploded in his mind: *Do seek Will for money.*

Do sequel for money?

Fandom Shrugged

Not by

Ayn Rand

W ho is Jean-Gault?"

The *Free Enterprise*'s senior officers were on the holodeck for their weekly game when the question arose. Deagna Troi was a counselor whose fierce intelligence and ambition overshadowed her lithe beauty and made many a man sorry he had underestimated her. She had acquired three of the game's four railroads and was trying to build herself an empire. Everyone who landed on one had to pay out seventy-five holocredits. When they complained she merely shrugged. "I earned these railroads," she would declaim, "and you are perfectly free not to roll the dice and land on them. Monopoly is the name of this game, and I am not ashamed to turn a profit."

Willful Rakehell was 6'3", with a strong brow and a resolve to match. A strong Will, Deagna sometimes jested. Rakehell owned the Rearding Railroad, but bad luck in his past had sent him directly to jail and he was hurting financially. Deagna kept offering exorbitant sums for the Rearding but Rakehell refused to sell. Instead he stood on the Community Chest on his next roll and talked for eleven uninterrupted and unparagraphed pages about private property and the privileges of ownership, but Deagna tuned him out until he summed up: "The man who acquires through the sweat of his brow knows what it truly is to own," he proclaimed, ignoring her offered fistfuls of holocredits.

"You could own me, Will," Deagna pronounced. "The strong woman is the woman who can relinquish control to the man who treats her like the bitch she really is. Sell me the Rearding."

They were on the upscale end of the holoboard, walking toward her swanky Park Place holopenthouse. He was wearing his metal top hat and she wore her silver thimble. In the distance were the computer-generated lights and sounds of the Boardwalk. Beyond that floated a red arrow and the word GO.

"I know your feelings for me," Rakehell held forth, "and that is why you must promise not to hate me for the things I will be compelled to do."

Deagna didn't understand, and over the next several turns it became clear that Rakehell had negotiated a secret deal with Beta and Whiff whereby they were paying him not to sell the railroad, in order to curtail Deagna's profits. In return Rakehell was included in the secret partnership of commercial holofactories being erected along Baratic Avenue, low-rent districts they were renovating. Deagna hated when her turn took her through this area. There was a crumbling old shuttle factory containing remnants of some kind of revolutionary warp engine. It was a sinister area populated by an illiterate and filthy holoproletariat begging for money and food. Holograms or not, nothing disgusted Deagna more than poor starving proles.

Deagna felt betrayed by Rakehell, and said as much to Beta when he went honking by in his shiny aluminum Italian sports car during his turn. Beta merely shrugged. "Who is Jean-Gault?" he asked rhetorically, and flicked his emotion chip out of the speeding car.

The question bothered Deagna. The mysterious identity of the true captain of the *Free Enterprise* was a source of constant speculation. Some said he was an alien. Some said there was no captain at all, but legends of his exploits persisted, a new one every week. Deagna felt that Commander Rakehell was the real power behind the *Free Enterprise,* and that many of the Federation regulations that had been passed to allow officers of inferior ability to rise in the ranks had been his lackey Beta's doing. Until recently Deagna had been proud of the fact that the people who ran the ship were better and smarter than the mewling helpless followers around them, and these elite used to enjoy gathering to drink expensive synthehol brandies and chortling over the useless and lifeless automatons over whom they had dominion.

But now there was something wrong with the ship, something no one had ever named or explained. And it had all begun with the question "Who is Jean-Gault?"

Deagna bent to recover the emotion chip Beta had discarded. It was a brand she had never seen before: plain white, with the United Federation of Planets logo stamped in gold on one edge.

It was Whiff's turn now and he came by glowering as he pushed his squeaking chromium baby carriage. Whiff was the tallest of the men and had the strongest brow, and naturally Deagna was very attracted to him. But the Klingon dealt in securities, and he had altered the game programming to allow himself to prosper in an illicit weapons trade based at his holdings on Khitomer Avenue. Deagna was certain he was the force behind the Short Line wreck she had suffered two turns ago. Earlier Whiff had earned 100 holocredits by winning a beauty contest.

"They have changed the rules again," Whiff grumbled. "The holocredits we are using are no longer based on the hologold standard."

Deagna was immediately alarmed. "Sell me your 'Get out of Brig Free' card," she demanded.

Whiff glowered. "You are the same as everyone else aboard this ship," he proclaimed. "No one speaks as much as declaims." He went on for another ten pages but she tuned him out until he finished: "The man who speaks in anything other than trite aphorisms is a selfless man. True leaders are self-made men."

"Hardly a tribute to unskilled labor," she replied wryly.

Now Rakehell came by in his metal top hat. Deagna was still stopped on the Hydrogen Works. The computer had wiped away a scenic forest, strip-mined, and blasted away holo-mountains to build this skeletal framework belching smoke. What a testament to human ambition, Deagna thought as she admired its vomiting smokestacks. Her heart swelled at this emblem of productive industry. Then Rakehell dinged his pewter hat politely at her and pointed out the Rakehell

Industries logo on the factory wall and she glowered. "This is my utility," he boasted. "Pay up."

"You can't build your own utility," she protested. "It's against the rules."

"The man of industry makes his own rules." He started to go on for another eight pages, but suddenly the gaming landscape faded around them, to be replaced with the bare white walls of the holodeck. At opposite corners stood Beta and Whiff.

"Computer," Beta commanded, "restore Monopoly Program C47."

The computer did not respond.

In the center of the holodeck a figure appeared. He wore officer's colors and captain's rank. He was short, slight, bald, and distinguished. Despite the fact that he was not tall and did not have much of a brow, there was a fierce intelligence and ruthless determination in his eyes that made Deagna want to give herself to him completely so that he could subjugate her in the way of a man who knows a woman's place in the world.

"For dozens of missions now," the figure spoke in an English accent, "you have been asking yourselves, Who is Jean-Gault? Well . . . you know those 'captains of industry' you hear so much about? I am one of them. Let me tell you exactly how I am so much better and smarter than all the rest of you. . . ."

He lectured for seven entire episodes about his superiority, and about how the worst kind of people in the galaxy were smart people who disagreed with him. He told everyone that the way to fix their interstellar economy and government was to stop having emotions because emotions were for animals and any idiot could have them, but smart people just disregarded them. "I swear," he concluded, "by my career and my love of it, that I will never act the part of another man, nor ask another man to act the part of mine."

Those receiving his voluminous diatribe might have transformed the Federation, but by this time they had either fallen asleep or switched to *Baywatch*.

Holodeck-5, or, God Bless You, Mr. Roddenberry

Not by
Kurt Vonnegut

he episode begins like this:

Listen: Commander Ditto has come unstuck in time. It ends like this: *Make it so.*

Human beings in the twenty-fourth century are much smarter than they are now. They think right thoughts and reach an agreeable consensus before they act. They use their primate hands to build faster-than-light vehicles that display every bit of the smart humans' origins as hunter-gatherers. Even though they are very smart and right-thinking, beneath their thin layer of forebrain that has made them civilized, they still have the instincts of hunter-gatherers and the brains of monkeys. They travel in clan-units and pay fealty to their vessel, which has been imbued with character and even given a name, much like a totem animal-god. They wear synthetic two-toned out-fits that identify one another as members of tribal units—stretchy things they must tug back in place every time they stand up.

No one said the future would be perfect.

One such warp-speed clan-unit built by these smarter future primates was the U.S.S. *Enterprise.* The *Enterprise* was named after a couple of earlier *Enterprises* that blew their fair share of cultures back into the stone age. This thoroughly modern *Enterprise* was carrying on a grand old tradition.

Carry on.

On a certain Tuesday in the twenty-fourth century the *Enterprise* found itself stuck in one of those convenient cosmic storms in the space-time continuum. These mysterious storms are everywhere in the future. Without them, fully half of the *Enterprise*'s adventures never would have occurred.

This particular storm was actually a clever ruse cooked up by the Rastafadorians, who were vague and slightly deific aliens with absolute mastery over the physical world. Even their dropped toast always landed butter-side up. The Rastafadorians had it in mind to kidnap a representative member of the human race in order to study us better because our actions made no sense to them.

It doesn't seem to have occurred to them that our actions make no sense to us either.

In any case, the Rastafadorians made one of the few boo-boos in their lengthy history, because the person they snatched during the space-time storm was Lieutenant Commander Ditto, a humanoid robot with no hunter-gatherer origins at all.

Ditto's name means "a duplicate or a copy. The same as stated before. Used to express sameness or agreement." Ditto certainly fit the bill, but was even smarter than the evolved hominids who surrounded him. Because he had none of the tribal culture or hunter-gatherer brains that impeded the thinking of his fellow clan members, he was enormously helpful in providing quick and straightforward solutions to difficult problems. Because he had no hormones or glands to color his judgement, his reasoning was unswayed by inferior emotions.

Everyone hated him.

Hate is a monkey emotion, you know.

Ditto quickly realized that the storm that had trapped the *Enterprise* was in fact an artificial phenomenon known as an idio-synchratic sesquipedalium. Since the storm was artificial, it had to have been generated for the purpose of kidnapping him. Therefore he was in the hands of vague and slightly deific aliens.

In reality, Ditto was incorrect about one of his assumptions.

Rastafadorians had no hands.

This is a commercial break:

Various multinational conglomerates make sincere and expensive attempts to make us desire products we have no use for. It's simply awful to go from this nifty ideal future to hemorrhoid medicines, but there's nothing to be done about it. It wouldn't be at all exaggerating to say that hemorrhoid medicines keep the *Enterprise* flying.

So, it goes.

Ditto's rank was Lieutenant Commander. In his holding cell on the Rastafadorian starship *Dreadlock,* Ditto explained the concept of rank to the puzzled Rastafadorians, who feel everyone is equal and the only creature in the universe better than any other is the One True God Marley. Ditto told the Rastafadorians that ranks are held because the Alpha Male in the primate order must be determined and the tribal hierarchy must be maintained. Even smarter primates recognize that episodic action-adventure cannot occur without conflicting hierarchies. It all comes from a book by the nineteenth-century human primate Charles Darwin entitled *On the Origin of Species* that has everything to do with smart primates and nothing whatsoever to do with this story.

Oh, well.

The name of the *Enterprise*'s Alpha Male was Jean-Luc Godard. Actually, the role of Alpha Male had been divided between two males, Godard and First Officer Wilhelm Von Reicher III, also known as Number One because he was number two in importance. Reicher handled hunter-gatherer expeditions known as "Away Team missions." He also displayed sexual dominance in his public galactic womanizing. Godard issued the primary tribal commands and assumed the mantle of experienced chieftain and wise man. Godard belonged to a religion called Vulcanonism, which preaches that religion is humbug and preaching is useless. Vulcanonists have no credo of faith, because they have a superstitious belief in the powers of science and logic. Vulcanonists vehemently despise strong emotions and have a dread fear of cowardice.

They only get laid once every seven years.

Reicher was a pagan but he didn't realize it, which quali-
fied him for the priesthood. Not realizing you are a pagan is
a prime requisite for unadulterated paganism. Reicher reli-
giously avoided church and was scrupulously amoral.

In talking to the Rastafadorians, Ditto realized that they
had become unstuck in time and were not developing as
superior creatures. Humans would probably catch up to
them by the seventh-inning stretch. The Rastafadorians
were too busy being deific to figure this out for themselves.

Ditto let them know what ninnies they were.

The Rastafadorians were pathetically grateful for this
revelation. They allowed Ditto to return to the *Enterprise*. It
wasn't really all that beneficent a gesture, because Ditto
wasn't a human and so he made their studies pretty much
useless.

Before they freed Ditto and released the *Enterprise* from
the chrono-simplistic infidelitum, though, the Rastafadorians presented Ditto with a fabulous message for his fellow
primate clansmen. This message was stored in Ditto's memory banks for that happy day when human beings were wise
enough to benefit by its timeless wisdom. It was the phrase
uttered by the Great God Marley, they told Ditto, the phrase
that had created the universe itself.

One day much later, as the crew flies, during a completely unrelated mission, Lieutenant Commander Ditto
received a subspace transmission about the Germulan fire-
bombing of the Dresden colony.

Dresden, he thought. Figures.

Immediately Ditto heard an internal electronic chirp, *po tee weet!,* and he plugged into his Science Station and the Rastafadorian message was broadcast throughout the ship and all over the Federation:

MAKE IT SO

Trek of Darkness

Not by

Joseph Conrad

The *Enterprise,* a Federation cruiser, eased to her berth in the space dock without a flutter of her impulse engines, and was at rest. The length of the Starbase stretched before her like the beginning of an interminable narrative. Beyond, the air was hazy where the bay entrance lay exposed to the eternal cosmos, held in by an invisible force field. Farther out, the mournful gloom of dark black space lay brooding darkly and blackly.

On the bridge we watched the Captain's back as he stood before the viewscreen looking spaceward, starlight gleaming on his bald pate. It threw a kind of light on everything, somber and not at all illuminating, a light that did not combat the darkness on the viewscreen. No. Yet his scalp reflected a kind of light. On all the channels there was nothing half so watchable. All of us on the bridge, the Captain, the First Officer, the Counselor, the Klingon, and myself, had taken up Space for the bulk of our lives. We stared placidly at the vast expanse of black that was like death, but death sprinkled with the dull shining of stars like souls engulfed by the gloomy black death of the inky morass of space which was like death.

"And this also," the Captain said suddenly, "is one of the dark places in the galaxy. I think of when the Romulans came

163

here, centuries ago. Imagine the feelings of a commander of a fine Bird of Prey, ordered suddenly to cross the dread black of space in a ship about as airtight as an old television plot, mingling with the utter savagery of the Gaullians he had been ordered to slaughter. No Ferengi wine here! The conquest of a planet, murder, slavery, subjugation. Those were grand days."

His remark was accepted in silence. We were accustomed to his lengthy ruminations.

"It was from this very dock that once I set out on the *Stargazer* on a crooked path paved with good intentions that led across the bridge over troubled waters which I burned behind me," he continued. The rest of us settled into our chairs; we knew we were fated to hear yet another of the Captain's inconclusive episodes.

"I was new aboard the *Stargazer* and still green, but I was summoned to this starbase to be briefed about a mission. On my arrival in Admiral D'Arqueness's office there were two Klingons waiting there. One petted a black tribble on his legs while the other pitched dice carved from black knucklebones. Often on my mission I thought of those two dark warriors guarding the door to D'Arqueness. They seemed a portent of something . . . dark.

"I was ordered to the Coppola Nebula, a brooding, murky morass of indeterminate content that remains a challenge to navigation even now. There I was to take charge of a two-credit oil transport, the *Nostromo*. On my way the *Stargazer* called in every outpost that sold synthehol. You would think that the ship ran on the stuff, and you would not be entirely incorrect.

"Once, just at the fringes of the nebula, we intercepted a garbled radio transmission from which we deciphered only a name: Kurtz. Could this, I wondered, be the near-mythical figure of Admiral Kurtz, long vanished under mysterious circumstances from Federation memory, consigned to legend and oblivion but rumored to be alive like some kind of Flying Dutchman whose career would not die peacefully?

"We followed this transmission to its source, and there we found the *Cairo,* an Excelsior-class ship commanded by Captain Jellico. There wasn't so much as an asteroid near her, yet she was firing photon torpedoes into empty space as if being attacked by the entire Cardassian fleet. She was in extreme disrepair and the whole proceeding was nothing short of insane. Jellico would not answer our hails, and the only reply we received to our demands that Jellico submit to our authority was a three-word message: 'Jelly don't serf.'"

Now the Klingon slowly rose and drew forth the ceremonial dagger bearing his family crest. As was the custom of his people, rather than break his iron control and endure public humiliation under the lash of this slow and torturous narrative, he quietly opened his veins and let the purple fluid of his life run out upon the deck.

The Captain gave no notice. "Continuing on my tiresome pilgrimage," he continued, "I plunged deeper into the inky cosmic jungle of that untamed nebula. We navigated past ejected warp cores, past corpses floating but surrounded by no trace of debris. We put in at an anarchic outpost staffed by indigenous aliens who were black-skinned and wore black clothing and wrote only in black ink. There was something . . . cheerless about them. There I learned that the *Nostromo* had been found floating, her crew and captain, Dallas, mysteriously dead, her escape pod jettisoned. I refurbished her with black-market equipment. During all this time there were many mysterious and sinister happenings, a phaser overloading, a communications satellite exploding, men found inexplicably hanged in zero gee, and at each instance the name of 'Kurtz' was uttered. One fuliginous night I asked a man, one of the few humans at the outpost, who was this mysterious Kurtz? 'He is the Admiral,' the man said. 'He is an emissary of science and progress and great drama, a Federation renegade who has made something of himself out here. All of us are influenced by Kurtz, even you, though you may not know it.'"

During the course of this narrative the life-support systems had begun to fail, and now it had become so pitch dark that we listeners—those of us surviving, for the Klingon was no longer breathing and the Counselor had cycled herself through the air lock without the encumbrance of a pressure suit—could hardly see one another. The Captain was no more than a voice, which I had long suspected anyhow. I continued to listen, looking for some clue to why his narrative gave me a sense of darkness and death.

"With my refurbished *Nostromo* and a motley crew of natives and outcasts I set out deeper into the Coppola Nebula," the Captain continued. "The journey was long and arduous and fraught with omens. Of it I will say little, if anything."

The First Officer had drawn his phaser and pointed it at himself. Now he breathed a great sigh of relief.

"At the center of the nebula was an immense black hole, a light-eating maw with nothing but darkness in its heart— say, that's a good image, don't you think? It was here, navigating through the treacherous debris field that had assembled around the gravity well of the singularity, that I found the station commanded by the man I had come to think of as my nemesis—Kurtz. We were near the accretion disk of the enormous black hole and condensed matter was thick as fog when our sensors became aware of the presence of small, two-man fighters of a primitive design not seen since the early days of space opera.

"These little fighters shot laughable, chemically ignited slugs at our ship as we passed them by. We took one of these ignorant fools prisoner by using the transporter to kidnap him. The ignorant blue savage thought he was dead, and gibbered to us as if we were welcome gods in his pagan afterlife. He was a member of the Ivry, a race entirely devoted to Admiral Kurtz, whom he claimed was a god. 'We are little men,' he ranted, 'he is a big man. We are nothing, and he is everything. He is smooth where we are hairy. His head is bald like yours, but polished and gleaming. He shakes the spear and talks the talk.' After a bout of this nonsense the deluded fellow put a spear through my finest officer, and damned if it didn't stain my uniform—the wretch!"

The First Officer, I saw in the dimness of the bridge, was now setting his phaser on highest power and maximum dispersion. When he saw that the Captain was going to continue, he turned the weapon on himself and pressed the firing stud. The glow of his extinction dispelled the gloom of the bridge, but then we were plunged again into the murk of the failing life-support systems. Better to curse the darkness, I thought.

"Not long after passing the Ivry curtain," the Captain continued, "the *Nostromo* sensed a damaged and half-dead shuttlecraft attempting to make its way from an uncharted planet in the region. There was a life-form aboard with barely registering life signs and we beamed it directly to our sickbay. Immediately our ship's doctor, an aging syntheholic with a boorish manner and quavering hands, notified me that I had better come take a look at his patient right away.

"The sight that greeted me in the sickbay was an image from Federation history. A decrepit and bald old man was gesturing hyperbolically as he argued with the doctor, whom he seemed to think was someone else. 'You . . . don't *understand,* Bones!' he delivered, staccato. 'You're . . . *violating* . . . my Prime Directive!' The man's ancient Federation uniform was of a stretchy design that looked remarkably uncomfortable as well as being a rather tacky mustard color.

It was torn and filthy. This superannuated relic's hyper-emotional voice, his histrionic delivery—I knew him! I had travelled halfway across the galaxy and deep into the black hole of deathly allegory to find—

"'Admiral Kurtz?'

"He looked stricken. 'Not Kurtz, damn you—Kirk! *Kirk!*' He struggled to rise but could not. The doctor discovered that tying the poor man's hands made him less vocal.

"'It's been you all this time, then,' I asked, 'directing these covert activities?'

"'All . . . I really wanted to do . . . was direct!' he gasped. 'I gave monologues—and those people *worshiped* me! But they turned against me! They made my star go nova! Those cling-on bastards, they killed my sun!' He clenched his fists and said this another five or six times.

"'He's been exposed to lethal levels of cathode radiation,' the doctor told me. 'His neural pathways are disintegrating. It's affected his speech and perspective until his universe is nothing more than props with him the only player. There's nothing I can do.'

"'That's horrible,' I said.

"Kirk freed his hands and rose to point at me. 'Horror! Horror! You . . . don't . . . know . . . horror! No matter how much I tried, all my life, they'd only let me be Kirk! *Captain* Kirk! Guest spots—voice-overs—a singing career—directing, producing—it didn't matter! For years they said I was dead! But in syndication, I . . . am . . . immortal! I . . . am . . . *Kirk!*'

"He settled back into the biobed and I thought then that he was gone. But he rallied himself enough to raise a quavering finger at me. Even at death's door he managed to suck in his gut. *'Get out now,'* he hissed. *'Before it's too late . . . for you!'*

"And then he was gone, and I looked into the future as I look out the viewscreen now, to see a universe—and a career—a bit less . . . bright . . . than before."

ON THE BRIDGE

Not by

Jack Kerouac

With the beaming-up of Dayta began the part of my life you could call my life on the bridge. Dayta was perfect for the bridge because he was made of it, which is to say he was a fast-thinking assemblage of super conductors and crazy software plugged directly into the Big and the All. I had heard of his inhuman antics and tremendous trials and tribulations that had led him all over the gonest galaxy and into the heart of some dark matter indeed.

I was hanging around the Zen-Forward trying to make some time with this curvy Benzadred chick Dearanna, who was empathic and so knew what was bubbling and fizzing in my warpspeed mind, when Geordie Parker happened to mention during a band break, as he was knocking spit out of his saxahorn, that he had heard that the *Zenterprise* had received a shipment of new data last night. It took me a moment to assimilate this.

Next thing you knew I had direct-beamed to the spotless cabin of the brand-spanking-new Commando Dayta, and there he stood, straightbacked and facing away from me with a screwdriver in his hand and a beautiful gleaming toaster on the counter in front of him. "Now, darling," he was saying, "here we are on the *Zenterprise,* and although when that Ferengi introduced us he told you we were

mechanically compatible and especially adaptable with lots
of plugs and sockets and so forth, it is absolutely necessary
now to postpone such mundane thoughts concerning our
recreational pleasures and remind you that you are, in fact,
merely a common kitchen appliance. . . . " and so on, in the
way he had in those happy crazed days before he had fully
integrated his ethic circuits.

I cleared my throat and introduced myself, and he lit up
and implored me to teach him all about the art of First Offi-
cering, and next thing I knew we were in the turbolift with
him saying "Bridge bridge bridge bridge," and on the bridge
for the first time in his career he strode across the deck as if
he owned it, looking at crazy consoles and lights flashing
with the promise of karmic possibility, and looking over
everyone's shoulder as they worked at their stations, and
yelling, "Fascinating! Interesting! Curious! Phew!" And at
the navigator's station he nearly threw the officer on duty
out of his seat with his mad gone enthusiasm, and he sat
down and turned off the automatic piloting controls one by
one until he was plugged directly in and it was just Dayta
and the *Zenterprise* in one beat fused hip technocreature
nanorgasmic being. He rode that seat like a cowboy on a
bronc, muttering the whole time phrases like "Dig these
soft consoles!" and "Affirmative affirmative affirmative, I
mean to say yes, sure, positively." His fingers danced like
crazy beautiful spiders on bennies as he disconnected the
impulse drive and pushed the warp drive an inhuman distance past her specs. The ship was redlined and moaning

and groaning, and Dayta was humming along with the ever-cosmic boom and bang. If he had sneezed, that ship would have caught a cold.

He located Geordie Parker blowing in the Zen-Forward Lounge like Neil and Louis Armstrong wailing the mating call of the Great Bird of the Galaxy, and Dayta whooped and patched it over the PA for everyone to dig and scope and assimilate. "I haven't had a wink of sleep since the day I was born," Dayta yelled over Parker's crazed-cat saxahorn wail, "and I mean to tell you in a manner of speaking that I've stolen, I should warn you, every kind of vehicle that ever left an atmosphere, searching all of space and finding out it's very big don't you know, which is I guess why they call it that, but never, *nada, nein* have I boosted so hot and all a ride as this, so smooth and automated it nearly drives itself and makes me wonder what it is all you swinging Fed cats do with your time, yaas, yaas, yaasss. . . ."

I asked what he was searching for and he turned his back to the zooming screen and the Holy Sensors and dodged an asteroid without looking while Geordie Parker's saxahorn wailed a crazy baby's warning on the P and A.

"Searching for?" He seemed amazed I didn't know. "Why—well—yes—I'm searching for the Big Answer, yaas, the secret at the heart of the universe, and nothing less will do!" He made the ship do the gonest flip barrel roll that engineers have since told me is impossible in a Galaxy-class boozer-cruiser, but I was there and he flipped it neat as a drugstore pimp with a silver dollar. "See, Will—ahem—we know the universe keeps on expanding and contracting in the greatest rolling wheel of karmic cycles, but to do that the whole universe needs to have a lot more mass than anyone's been able to find, and none of those chrome-dome Federation eggheads can figure out where this missing mass might be, which is what makes it so *missing,* you dig?"

He slapped the console and sat up. "Whew!—ahem—yes. It is exactly eighteen hundred hours, Will. I will lock the controls for our return at exactly, let us say, twenty-one hundred hours."

"Where are we going?" I asked.

We made our prolific and roundabout way to the bar, stopping along the way to break into the sickbay. "Ahem—well, well—let us fill our pockets, in the metaphorical sense because of course we have no pockets, with manna morphine and dexterous dexadrine and beneficent bennies," and no sooner did the great god Dayta speak than it was accomplished, all hands on Dex and sounding the Reds Alert.

With our sensors on maximum we stumbled through the dimlit drowsy humdrum decks like ragged prophets in search of the missing mass, but finding instead a Massive Miss in the form of our own Benzadred Counselor Dee Dee "Double-D" Stroi. We hooked out our hopeful thumbs but the only ride she gave us was the bum's rush, and so we stumbled laughing and crazy with our heads turned back to watch her own bum rush sternly, which is to say toward the rear.

The Zen-Forward was lit amphetamine-bright and the sounds of the music and patrons calling zoom and boom and whoom were jazzing up the room. Geordie Parker puckered playing pipes for pickled patrons, all visored cool in his crazy jazzman shades. Beside him "Doc" Soos walloped the rollicking keypad with a cigarette in her hangdog countenance, swaying slow and lazy with a tragic and gloomy voice and a Mona Lisa smile to utter untold Buddha secrets: "Socks in box," she told the mike, and Geordie jammed toot-toot. "Locks on box," and the Doctor tickled tink-tink. "Jocks in frocks, flocks that groks."

Dayta snapped his fingers hard enough to make sparks fly. The whole scene was mad in the hatterest of ways. We drank whiskey till things got hazy and there was an incident I can't quite recall—two Klingon girls—and I was thinking of going to the coatroom to check for loose wallets when in walked Fearless Leader, Big Daddy-o himself, Beat Captain Ken-Luc Kesey. Dayta leapt to his feet and met him in the middle of the room. "Dig him, man!" he proclaimed, and began rubbing the captain's bald head until it made mousy squeaks that somehow blended with the ghost jazz haunting around them. "Isn't he the finest sweetest cat in the galaxy! Dig that shiny Buddha head, that turtleneck leonine leotard so amazing in its stretch simplicity! I mean, really look at him and dig him, daddy!"

"Mr. Dayta, I presume." Ken-Luc was cool as a frozen cat and did not even blink. "I understand you've locked the navigational controls."

"Yaas—well—ahem—I have not *locked* so much as freed the *Zenterprise* to head where its positronic heart most yearns to go, without, you see, the distraction of human interference."

The captain would have thrown him in the brig right then, I think, but at that moment the room was cut by a piercing howl that somehow blended with the techno jazz engineered by Mr. Geordie Parker himself. We looked to the stage to see the mad Klingon, Alien Worfsburg, striking a dramatic pose with maddened eyes and a clenched fist and a sheet of paper with the magic-markered title "Hurl" trembling in his big brown warrior-poet hand. "I saw the best minds of the next generation destroyed by expositional declaiming," he declaimed as the ivories chuckled along behind him, "weary trekkers looking for an angry fix."

"Hey, could you chill, man?" hollered "Doc" Soos. "I'm trying to modulate!"

Everyone applauded, and Worfsburg hurried from the stage with an angry clash of his finger cymbals.

Right then the Red Alert sounded and Dayta explained that, well, you see, we had reached what might be called our final destination which he had programmed, which objective was the very heart of our veriest galaxy, and with a whoosh and a bang we all found ourselves whisked from the bar to a state road on some gone alien planet somewhere, standing on a prairie under a blue blue sky without a vehicle in sight. Blind old Geordie Parker kept right on blowing. "Doc" Soos wasn't there, but Geordie never missed a Beat.

Ken-Luc Kesey got so red he looked like a thermometer dropped into boiling oil and he started hollering at Dayta that this was the ultimate hay, the last straw. Dayta only scratched and shrugged and wrinkled his crazy white forehead and pointed up at the sky when Ken-Luc was done.

We all looked up and the clouds parted and a face appeared all lit up like the sun, and verily it spoke unto us, saying, "Me Q. Who you? You Q? Q you!" And thus the face grew angry and spake downward, "You should blow! Do not pass GO! Make it so!"

And lo! were we expelled from Galactic Central Adam and Eve–like to wander the wondering spaceways and fly the fiendly skies for forty prolific days and forty terrific nights committing the seven deadly syndication seasons and hitching rides with Cardassian cargo haulers and tribble traders until we could find our way back to Headeration Fedquarters, where I try and try to type our travels and travails on a keypad that lets me run on and on because it never needs the paper changed but also seems to have broken "return" and "indent" keys—not to mention erratic punctuation—and as I realize that I'm running out of jazz CDs to type along with I think of Dayta, who last I heard had tuned in his logic circuits and turned on his emotion chip and dropped out of Federation space to land a gig piloting an ancient sublight passenger transport for Ken-Luc Kesey and the Merely Pranksters. I wonder where he is now in the space-filled galaxy missing all that mass. I wonder but I just don't know because I don't have enough data, I need more data, I need more Dayta.

Oh, the Treks You'll Take!

Not by
Dr. Seuss

The whole thing began
In the Transporter Room
When the Transporter Chief
Beamed up a ZLAGOON!

We shot it with phasers
And sang a cantata,
But it didn't stop
Till we fed it raw data!

It detoured into
The Ten-Forward Lounge
And drank every bottle
Of booze it could scrounge!

It drank Vulcan brandy,
And Cardassian ale.
It drank crème de cacao
From a ten-gallon pail!

It finally stumbled
On Holodeck 5,
And Jordy's quick thinking
Gave hope we'd survive.

He programmed with Barkley,
They programmed till noon,
Until they created . . .

A FEMALE ZLAGOON!

We thought they'd be happy,
Mrs. Z and her beau,
But their failed plasma coupling
Caused the warp core to blow!

BOOM!

—The End

ACKNOWLEDGMENTS

Wunderkind grunge prophet Lauren Horwitch wrote initial drafts of "The Crusher in the Rye," "Even Captains Get the Blues," and "On the Bridge." Trexpert Lanny Fields wrote an initial draft of "Trek of Darkness." Though I made extensive revisions, a great deal of what is funny in those pieces is entirely their material.

Über-testaroso Brian Livesay coined the word "schwoopy." Long may it wave.

Cartoonist/animator and all-around genius Ken Mitchroney drew the Dr. Seuss illustrations for "Oh, the Treks You'll Take!"

Renaissance woman Jessie Horsting did engine work and minor repairs—as usual.